M000223127

DEPLOY EMPATHY

A PRACTICAL GUIDE TO INTERVIEWING CUSTOMERS

MICHELE HANSEN

DOTSQUARE PRESS

Copyright © 2021 Michele Hansen.

All rights reserved.

Cover design by Damien Terwagne.

Scripts, templates, and phrasing may be used in customer conversations, emails, or other direct customer interactions without attribution. (For the purposes of this notice, "customer" refers to a person who currently, previously, or who could plausibly pay for or use a product or service.)

Any public or presentation contexts, such as posting to a blog, newsletter, podcast, talk, presentation, book, or other situations that are not direct customer interactions require attribution.

Using, adapting, and sharing the scripts within a company or consultant-client relationship is permitted and indeed encouraged. In the case of a consultant-client relationship, attribution is required.

I hate wasting time and writing code that never gets used. The only way I've found to truly avoid that when building my SaaS apps is to talk to the people I want to have as customers. *Deploy Empathy* takes the anxiety out of having these conversations so you can get honest thoughts about what you're trying to accomplish.

- MICHAEL BUCKBEE, FOUNDER, EXPEDITED SECURITY

Deploy Empathy is an essential field guide for anyone working close to product and customers. The book is filled with practical advice on customer interviews with Michele's unique ability to not just explain the how but also the equally important why. Learning from her experience is like taking a master class in nurturing product insights out of potential and existing customers. There is truly something for everyone involved in the product lifecycle.

- JOSH HO, FOUNDER, REFERRAL ROCK

Over the last 15 years, I've helped developers sell software and marketers to build software. Convincing them to talk to customers and really listen to customer problems has always been a challenge. *Deploy Empathy* is the instruction manual for customer interviews I've always wanted. Finally, I can direct my clients to scripts and techniques they can use to learn more directly from their customers. Many of them would have saved months, some hundreds of thousands of pounds, had they applied the practices in this book.

- JONATHAN MARKWELL, SMALL SAAS ADVISOR, PLAINSCALING

Michele's expertise and knowledge in customer interviews have been instrumental in shaping the way we launch new products and features. Before reading *Deploy Empathy*, I thought I was pretty good at talking with our users and translating those conversations into useful features. After applying some of her interviewing techniques, the feedback has become so much richer and illuminating. It is helping to shape our long term strategic objectives, not just setting immediate goals.

- MATTHEW LEHNER, CO-FOUNDER & CTO, ONEFEATHER

Doing customer interviews right is an art. It takes practice and skill to think on your feet to ask the right questions. Michele nails it on her podcast, *Software Social*, and especially in this book. I'm a long-time believer in talking to customers, and now I feel I have the techniques to get the best results.

- ROB BAZINET, FOUNDER, STILL RIVER SOFTWARE

"If I can do this, you can."

Apparently, the first time I uploaded data to Geocodio was June 28, 2016, so that had to be the year I experienced my first customer interview with Michele. I wonked out on her about pulling in Census data. Now, I'm the smallest of small-time users until now because my products didn't launch, but I'm building my third one and it looks like this bird will fly.

So, who did I track down to follow and emulate? Michele Hansen of Geocodio. What did I find? Her advice on doing customer research—a task that always made me meltdown whenever I thought about it. Her advice helped me understand that I'm actually excited to do customer research because I love talking about the problem with this product because I am receiving responses from people who actually feel the pain my product will relieve. Maybe one day I'll graduate to a gentle tone and simple questions, but until then I'm looking forward to culling the information I learn while talking to them.

- ANDREA BRICE, TECHNICAL HEAD AND FOUNDER OF WILLOWFINCH

In an ever-increasing automated world, *Deploy Empathy* is a humane, practical, and actionable manuscript, full of tools you can use right away to listen to your customers with empathy. It is a solid way to make better-informed business decisions all while turning customers into advocates.

- DAMIEN TERWAGNE, CO-FOUNDER, DAWN

Michele's writing is amongst the very best in the SaaS space at the moment. It's different. Where other books teach the "what works," *Deploy Empathy* will put you in your customers' shoes and teach you the all-important "why" behind what you're asking. As a developer who is currently attempting to validate a few ideas, understanding exactly how to approach people in a way that doesn't come across as a hardcore sales pitch has been a massive help, and this book gives you the exact words and techniques you need to use to get the best results. Without a doubt, *Deploy Empathy* has already saved us countless hours of coding something nobody actually wants.

- DARIAN MOODY, ENGINEERING LEAD AND CO-FOUNDER OF A COMPANY IN THE DISCOVERY PHASE

Deploy Empathy is a delightful resource for anyone who needs to get people to share sophisticated, important things about their work and business. It is a showcase of clever, fundamental, and—most importantly—learnable conversation skills.

Before reading *Deploy Empathy*, I thought that a long silence in an interview was an awkward pause. But Michele taught me that silence is just the sound that tremendously valuable information makes just before it arrives. Since reading the book, I've begun to revel in the so-called awkward pause, instead of fearing it.

- DANIEL BECK, FREELANCE TECHNICAL WRITER

This book prompted me to have my first customer call, and I learned so much! I found myself wanting to insert my own thoughts and opinions so many times—I didn't realize how often I did that until I consciously held back. But I did hold back, and it resulted in my customer opening up a whole lot more. Mirroring and summarizing is also such a power move. *Deploy Empathy* has been so helpful already, and this is only the beginning.

- ADAM MCCREA, FOUNDER, RAILS AUTOSCALE

CONTENTS

PART 7
INTERVIEWS

PART 8
ANALYZING INTERVIEWS

PART 9
PULLING IT ALL TOGETHER: SAMPLE INTERVIEW

PART 10
WHAT NOW?

APPENDIX B: FOR FOUNDERS

[PART 1]
USING THIS BOOK

[1]
EMPATHY IS A LEARNABLE SKILL

Your time is too valuable to spend it creating things people don't want.

As counterintuitive as it may seem, talking to people can save you months or years of frustrating, fruitless effort.

You might be afraid that talking to customers (or potential customers) will be a waste of time. That they will only tell you things you already know. Or, worse, that it will be awkward and you'll accidentally offend people.

That's okay.

But you also might be looking for new opportunities. You might be wondering why people cancel. You might be wondering how to get more people to buy. You might be trying to figure out which features to add next. And your data may not be giving you clear answers.

A spreadsheet of data can tell you *what* is happening, but it will never tell you *why*.

This is where adding customer interviews to your skillset can help.

This book will teach you how to deploy empathy in a specific, targeted, and structured way to pull opportunities out of customers that you and your competitors didn't even realize were there. People will tell you things—useful, actionable things—that you never would have found before.

Even if you have never interviewed customers before.

Even if your company doesn't exist yet.

Even if your company has been around for decades.

Even if you don't think you have time for interviews and only talk to customers in support or sales settings.

The skills you will learn can be used with potential customers, former customers, current customers, clients, stakeholders, people you advise, and even in your personal life.

You will walk away from this book with a toolbox of repeatable processes that will allow you to find opportunities and moments of unexpected insight time and time again.

The opportunities you find can be used across any part of a business—from what to write on landing pages to which features to prioritize to what kind of pricing model to choose to who your real competitors are.

To find those opportunities, you will first learn a set of conversation techniques that will help you listen with empathy and intention. It's okay if the ways of speaking presented in this book are unfamiliar to you. While it may come naturally to some, for many empathy is a learned skill.

But before you learn how to deploy empathy in customer interviews, let's address a common objection. Interviewing customers may sound squishy and subjective. It may sound like a "nice to have" rather than a critical part of a business.

So don't just take my word for it.

Writer Morgan Housel, one of the best business writers of our time, wrote in *The Psychology of Money*:

> "In a world where intelligence is hyper competitive, and many previous technical skills have become automated,

competitive advantages tilt toward nuanced and soft skills, like communication, empathy, and perhaps most of all, flexibility."[1]

Fortunately, anyone can learn the skills mentioned by Housel. According to Brené Brown, "Empathy is best understood as a learned skill, because being empathetic, or having the capacity to show empathy, is not a quality that is innate or intuitive."[2]

WHAT IS EMPATHY?

As defined by design strategist Indi Young in *Practical Empathy*, empathy is "about understanding how another person thinks, and acknowledging [their] reasoning and emotions as valid, even if they differ from your own understanding."

In this context, empathy means entering the other person's world and understanding that their decisions and actions make sense from their perspective. As put plainly by former FBI Chief Hostage Negotiator Chris Voss in *Never Split the Difference*, "The beauty of empathy is that it doesn't demand you agree with the other person's ideas."[3] It is similar to the concept of "beginner's mindset": suspending your own preconceived notions before entering a situation to uncover new information that you would not have come across had you kept only your own ideas in mind. This suspension of judgment is critical for finding problems that you may not have realized existed.

Learning empathy alone—aside from applying it to product development, marketing, and business strategy—is also something that can make you a better leader. According to Brené Brown, "In the growing body of empathy research, we are finding that successful leaders often demonstrate high levels of empathy; that empathy is related to academic and professional success; that it can reduce aggression and prejudice and increase altruism." [4]

I encourage you to try these techniques with friends and family before talking to customers. With practice, the listening techniques and frameworks you'll find in this book will become second nature.

It is worth taking a moment to differentiate between empathy, sympathy, and solution-based responses. For example, if someone says, "My boss yelled at me today!" a sympathetic response would be "I'm sorry that happened to you" (which creates distance between the original speaker and the person replying), and a solution response would be "You should get a new job," which comes from a good place yet changes the subject away from the person's experience. By contrast, an empathetic response might be "That really hurt you," which encourages the person to expound on their experience. Regardless of your natural inclination, it is my belief that everyone is capable of adding empathetic responses and exploration paths to their communication toolbox.

EMPATHY FOR CUSTOMERS HELPS COMPANIES OF ALL SIZES

Your customers (or potential customers) have a wealth of insights for you, and you just need to ask them.

When you understand the details of why and how someone embarks on a process, you can then see where opportunities may lie.

That awareness of more opportunities—from new products to marketing existing ones to strategy and more—is why more and more companies have integrated listening to customers directly into their decision-making processes.

Payment processor Stripe is a notable example. According to Stripe product manager Theodora Chu, "at Stripe, the very first question you'll get for any product proposal is, 'Who are the users, and what do they care about?'" Stripe not only integrates customer research into the core of their decision-making, they also encourage entire teams—developers included—to interview customers directly.

I've had the privilege of being interviewed by their product managers, developers, and designers myself. Says Chu, "you're expected to talk to users throughout your time at Stripe, regardless of function."[5]

You'll read vignettes from Stripe's customer research practices throughout this book, as well as examples from my own company, Geocodio, and from founders at different stages. What all of these companies have in common—from small side projects to one of the most admired technology companies in the world—is that customers are integrated into their decision-making and everyday work processes.

Unfortunately, actively listening to customers is a resource that many companies overlook. Many large businesses have research arms, yet they are often insulated from the rest of the company. There is substantial value in having developers, product managers, marketers, and other functions—besides researchers—interview and interact with customers. Companies that insulate research—or, worse, neglect it entirely—leave that valuable resource completely untapped to their own detriment.[6] But that, in turn, creates an opportunity for competitors that are willing to do the work to understand customers.

You are therefore creating an advantage for your company just by having empathy for your customers and being open to listening to them.

[2]

THE NEUROSCIENCE OF LISTENING

Over the thousands of interviews I've conducted, I've found that customers we interview tend to become our most vocal supporters. The customers we've interviewed go on to be the ones who passionately share the word in their networks. The customers we've interviewed are the most likely to offer to do a testimonial, even without us asking.

Most of us are so used to being ignored by companies that when we find one that listens to us—and genuinely listens to us—it's startlingly refreshing. It makes people want to go out of their way to see that company succeed.

There is a deeper neurological reason why this happens.

According to functional magnetic resonance imaging brain studies, parts of the brain associated with motivation, reward, and enjoyment light up when people talk about themselves and their experiences with another person.[1]

Being listened to makes people feel happy, and the person talking associates those positive feelings with the person and concept they're talking about. In the case of a customer interview, that means those happy feelings get transferred to you and in turn, your company.

The mere act of listening alone is powerful. I want you to

remember that study when you find yourself wondering whether you're asking the right questions, your interviews are long enough, or whether you're analyzing them in the right way. (Later on, we'll address each of those concerns.)

Just listening to customers alone has benefits for you and your company. Even if you do nothing with what you've learned afterward.

[3]
WHY I WROTE THIS BOOK

People often ask me how my husband and I have been able to grow our software company, Geocodio, to over one million dollars in annual revenue without external funding.

Do you want to know the secret?

Here it is: listening to customers is embedded in everything we do. Listening to customers is the cornerstone, foundation, and pillars of how we make decisions. By listening to customers and learning their processes, we learn how to get and retain customers by helping them accomplish things faster, cheaper, and easier.

Hearing that, people then wanted to learn how to interview customers themselves. I didn't feel like I had one solid place to send them, and I would find myself typing out long emails that were a mix of chapters of books, podcasts, and blog posts, with my own perspectives spliced in. (As you'll learn in this book, repeated manual work like that is a symptom of pain that can be solved by a product. In this case, a book.)

Most resources on customer research are only partly relevant to people trying to start or grow businesses and are written for user experience professionals. I needed a resource that presumed no previous experience with customer research and was also biased toward action.

This book is specifically intended to fill two gaps in the existing (and wonderful) body of work on customer research, much of which I reference throughout this book.

The first is specific words, phrases, and scripts to use when talking to customers, whether in an interview setting or support setting. Many books mention phrases and tactics, yet they often do not get into the nitty gritty of exact questions to ask in specific situations to the extent that would be needed by someone who has zero customer research training. The idea of this book is that, if you had to, you could read How to Talk So People Will Talk to get an idea for how to get people to open up, and then take one of the scripts into an interview with only minor adjustments. It is designed to be grab-and-go.

Second, with the exception of *The User Experience Team of One*, many of the books on user research are written with large, well-resourced teams in mind.

If you're in a team setting, I suggest using this book in tandem with *The Jobs to Be Done Playbook* by Jim Kalbach. Steve Portigal's *Interviewing Users* is excellent for those who have the resources and ability to meet with customers in person. Consultants might look to Erika Hall's *Just Enough Research*, which is written from a design agency perspective.

This book attempts to make customer research methods accessible to even the smallest of companies—including companies of one, in software entrepreneur Paul Jarvis' words.

Paul Jarvis' *Company of One* is one of the most influential books in the world of small software companies. Rob Walling's *Start Small, Stay Small* and Arvid Kahl's *Zero to Sold* are also part of that canon.

The sparking motivation for this book was to offer a way to help founders and prospective founders, often developers, run their own companies with customer understanding built into the core of their decision-making process. Building products and features that people don't want is *painful* and if people knew how to talk to customers and potential customers to get useful information, they wouldn't have to go through that.

Trying to introduce customer perspectives into the product development process later on in a company's lifecycle can be painful, too.

Anyone who has tried to introduce customer research into a company that makes decisions without talking to customers knows just how much of a slog it can be.

Cindy Alvarez's *Lean Customer Development* is written from the perspective of a product manager and has specific tips for introducing customer research into a resistant organization. If you are in that situation and have skeptical higher-ups, read Alvarez's book yourself and try to get your leadership to read one of Clayton Christensen's books, which are written from a high-level, executive-friendly perspective.

But what if more companies were built with customer empathy from the very beginning? Retrofitting customer research into the organization wouldn't be necessary, because it would already be baked in.

In the early days of Stripe, founders Patrick and John Collison personally answered support emails and watched users integrate the product.

According to Stripe product manager Theodora Chu, "they built up a strong sense of 'What do developers want? And how do we make our APIs better by virtue of spending time with developers and watching how they use our APIs." As a result, user research is something that's "baked into Stripe's DNA" because it's been there from day one.

And it still is for new employees. "One of the first things you do when you join Stripe is you try and answer a support ticket, and you try and help a user through their pain point...We care a lot about people who are focused on users in general. You're expected to talk to users throughout your time at Stripe, regardless of function."[1]

It is my grand ambition to help people learn how to listen to customers and integrate it into their workflow from the start. While they are only one group of readers of this book, I believe that developers and makers are the next huge wave of founders. Demystifying the skills to pull wants and needs out of potential customers would save them hours, months, and years of pain.

HOW I GOT STARTED WITH ALL OF THIS

Before I was a software entrepreneur, I was a product manager at a mid-size company. We'd look at analytics and talk to customer service and then make educated guesses about what we needed to do to a product to get the metrics to go in the right direction.

Even though I was a frequent visitor in the customer service department, it never occurred to me that we could talk to customers directly.

I remember the first time someone suggested the idea of user testing our products before we launched them. "How are we supposed to find time for that?" I thought to myself. A week of user testing and then another two weeks of tweaking based on that feedback just wasn't in the cards for our hectic four-to-six week product launch cycles.

It was only later, as my mind became more open to qualitative research and I had my own "Aha!" moments while talking to customers that I learned that it is absurd to start customer research the week before launch—because it needs to happen much sooner, as part of guiding the development of the product.

I saw for myself how it can improve product roadmaps, increase team motivation, and get numbers moving in the right direction.

Talking to customers was a revelation.

Practicing and applying empathy didn't come naturally to me, and it's something I've had to learn.[2] I was fortunate enough to learn customer research under the wing of an experienced design leader and a PhD user researcher. I observed their interviews for months before conducting my own.

It took me a long time to realize the value that can come from listening to customers and how to do so in a way that leads to results, and I try to keep that in mind whenever I'm talking about this.

If you're new to this, you may not believe me until you start seeing the results and having those "Aha!" moments of learning for yourself. I recognize that interviewing customers and integrating them into your decision-making is a mental leap for a lot of people.

Let's embrace your doubt. I accept that you may be worried that this will be a waste of time. If you follow the methods outlined in this book, you will get useful feedback out of your interviews and you can stop spending time on things that people don't want. You'll get there, and this book is your step-by-step guide.

[4]

WHAT THIS BOOK CAN HELP YOU DO

Perhaps you find yourself, either now or at other times, needing to do one of the following:

- Launch a product
- See if people would pay for something
- Understand why people are canceling
- Know why people *are* buying, so you can find more customers
- Determine which features to add next
- Figure out how to keep customers and why people buy again

If any of those apply to you, this book is for you.

This book is intended to make the tribal knowledge about talking to users that is largely constrained to the user research community accessible to a much broader audience.

This book is written for people who do not come from a user experience background. That includes everyone from developers to product managers to marketers to founders.

If you do have experience with interviewing, this book's primary usefulness to you may be as a resource to recommend to developers, product managers, and other team members as an introduction to interviewing that is approachable yet rigorously grounded.

This book is in part inspired by a line in veteran user researcher Steve Portigal's book *Interviewing Users*: "Much of this presumes that the fieldwork team is assembled from two types of people: those who are likely to be reading this book, and those who wouldn't even have imagined a book like this existed." This book is written with that latter group in mind. It is intended to be an approachable introduction that is heavy on practical application.

---

[5]

HOW THIS BOOK IS STRUCTURED

This book is organized linearly. It starts with mental models for thinking about customer problems, to figuring out when to do research, to recruiting participants, to preparing for interviews and creating a script, then to analyzing interviews and taking action.

But just because this book is organized linearly doesn't mean you need to read it linearly. This is intended to be a practical guide, so feel free to skip around and make it useful for yourself. (See Appendix A for the non-linear reading guide.)

PART II: KEY FRAMEWORKS

There are several underlying ideas and mental models that are referenced throughout this book. This book isn't heavy on theory, yet it's important to have these highly-actionable models in mind as you conduct and analyze interviews.

PART III: GETTING STARTED

Customer interviews are very, very different from the interviews you might observe in daily life. It's more like how a therapist talks to their patients than a journalist on TV.

This part is a step-by-step guide to interviewing like a user researcher would and will help you build up your skills before talking to prospective, current, and former customers or clients.

If you've already interviewed a customer or ten, you can probably skip this section and go right on to Part IV.

PART IV: WHEN SHOULD YOU DO INTERVIEWS?

This section introduces a mental model for thinking about when to do interviews: project-based research (when you have a specific problem you're trying to figure out) and ongoing research (for building and updating your general understanding of customer needs). I use this framework for my own research, and it's also used by Stripe.[1] You'll find your own research flow, and I present this model as a starting point to help you figure out when interviews are the right tool for the job.

PART V: RECRUITING PARTICIPANTS

The next part walks you through one of the biggest challenges for people at first: finding people to talk to, especially if you don't have any customers. You'll get specific copy to use to find interview participants on Reddit, Twitter, LinkedIn, Facebook, and email lists. If you already have customers, it includes copy and questions to use via email and short surveys.

PART VI: HOW TO TALK SO PEOPLE WILL TALK

How to Talk So People Will Talk is the most important part of this book.

Interviews are more like acting than a conversation, and this part will teach you specific tactics to use to help people open up and talk about relevant topics.

If you are pressed for time, read this part and then skip to Appendix A to get power packs for specific situations.

PART VII: INTERVIEWS

This is the part you will probably reference the most in the future: the essentials of interviewing. This part gets into the nuts and bolts of interviews and includes scripts for specific scenarios (like cancellation interviews, testing a prototype, or when you're in the early stages and exploring a problem). It also includes deep dives on specific questions, like how to ask someone what they would pay.

If you're one to skip around: Do not start using the scripts before reading How to Talk So People Will Talk.

Interviews don't always go according to plan, and that's okay. In the last chapter of this part, "Debugging Interviews," you'll get guidance on what to do in some common situations and how to recover.

PART VIII: ANALYZING INTERVIEWS

After that, it's time to dive into analysis methods. This part will introduce you to a simplified version of a customer journey map (it's okay if you don't know what that is) and a matrix for determining which problems and tasks might be good opportunities.

PART IX: PULLING IT ALL TOGETHER: SAMPLE INTERVIEW AND ANALYSIS

This section shows you the interview tactics in action and walks through different ways of analyzing interviews, including a long-form version and an analysis for when you're low on time.

PART X: WHAT NOW?

Here, you'll find further resources. This book has a narrow focus on the interview skills and tactics that are glossed over in other books. Accordingly, there are a lot of important topics that are intentionally excluded, and this part is a launchpad for exploring those other topics.

APPENDIX A: CHEAT SHEET

Appendix A is your handy guide to skipping around this book. Trying to figure out what to build? Need to know why people cancel? This section has power packs of chapters for specific purposes to make it easy to get the answers you need and get to work.

APPENDIX B: FOR FOUNDERS

Appendix B is specifically for founders of small software companies. It includes discussion of common customer support situations, turning feature requests into research, the differences between support, sales, and research, and one way to use customer research as part of goal setting.

[PART 2]
KEY FRAMEWORKS

The underlying idea of this book is that you can deploy empathy to uncover the process a customer is going through and in turn use that understanding to help you make business decisions.

This section starts with an overview of the process-based approach and presents three key frameworks that are referenced throughout the book:

- The core questions to answer in an interview
- The three dimensions of a process: Functional, social, and emotional
- Valuable, usable, viable, and feasible

Understanding these frameworks will help you structure your thinking about customer interviews and guide you as you think about which questions to ask, how to ask follow-up questions, and what do with what you learn.

[6]
EVERYTHING IS A PROCESS

Think about these common tasks for a moment:

- Doing laundry
- Filing taxes
- Making coffee or tea in the morning

Chances are, they show up on your mental to-do list as one item, but they're really a combination of tasks rolled up together. They are *processes*. And they take different amounts of time, require different tools, and have different amounts of complexity. You might solve them differently based on how much time you have, who else is involved, and how you're feeling that day.

Compared to each other, those tasks all have different frequencies too. Doing laundry is much more frequent than doing taxes. Making coffee is more frequent than doing laundry.

And depending on context, you may be willing to pay for a product that makes steps of that process easier or eliminates them entirely. Sometimes people think they need to solve the entire process in order to create something others would buy. This is sometimes the case, but due to the complexity that goes into even "simple" tasks, making just one step easier, faster, or cheaper can make a huge difference for people.

Laundry detergent pods eliminate the relatively trivial step of measuring out laundry detergent. That trivial step is now a nine billion dollar annual global market.[1]

The idea of this book is that you can use empathy to uncover the process for a particular goal and use that understanding to help you make business decisions (including product, marketing, engineering, sales, pricing, and more).

People are more willing to pay to solve problems that are frequent, and people are more willing to pay to solve problems that are complex, time consuming, expensive to get wrong, or otherwise frustrating in some way.

Understanding the steps of a process and the functional, social, and emotional dimensions that lead someone to choose a particular route can uncover opportunities: for product creation, marketing, pricing, and more.

This process-based understanding can enable you to see which steps are frequent and painful, which correlates with willingness to pay. Making one (or several) of those steps easier, faster, or cheaper can help you build the right product and in turn a thriving, happy customer base.

I use "build" here liberally. It does not require that you are in the beginning stages of a company, and these same tactics can be used to reboot the marketing for a struggling product.

Empathy can be used throughout the entire business lifecycle, from deciding which products to build, to what pricing model to use, to how to treat people in customer support settings, and more.

Starting to notice that many tasks are processes in your daily life will help you as you interview customers.

It will help you know when to dig deeper when someone says something that they regard as one task but is really a package of tasks, like "sending an invoice" or "scheduling a meeting."[2]

Every task is a process.

Every process is situational.

[7]

THE CORE QUESTIONS

You can use the scripts and templates in this book a starting point for your own interviews. The scripts build off a set of core questions:

1. What are they trying to do overall?
2. What are all of the steps in that process?
3. Where are they now?
4. Where does the problem you are solving fit in that process?
5. Where in that process do they spend a lot of time or money?
6. How often do they experience this problem?
7. What have they already tried?

This book is not heavy with theory, but it is grounded in the Jobs to Be Done framework. It is a way of conceptualizing why people "hire" and "fire" specific products based on the overall goal they're trying to achieve and the context within which they are accomplishing that goal.

For example, someone may grind coffee beans (*task*) to make themselves a cup of coffee (a collection of tasks, i.e., *activity*) to be able to focus on their work (*goal*).

That larger goal is similar to what Kathy Sierra in *Badass: Making Users Awesome* calls the "Compelling Context." It's the big reason why someone does something in the first place.

Someone doesn't drink coffee *just* because they enjoy the taste or *just* because they want to focus on work. They may also want to seem competent to their coworkers and avoid getting fired.

From that perspective, an individual product is inevitably only one (or two) steps in that process toward a larger goal. Products that solve multiple steps allow people to accomplish the goal faster, cheaper, or easier, leading to higher customer satisfaction and all of the ensuing benefits (higher lifetime value, word-of-mouth, and so forth).

Kathy Sierra's *Badass* is an excellent introduction thinking about user experience and marketing around the user's broader goals rather than the features of the product.

Jobs to Be Done was pioneered by the late Harvard Business School professor Clayton Christensen and marketing consultant Bob Moesta. Its intellectual grounding comes from the academic field of activity theory, which was first developed in the 1930s. Jim Kalbach's *The Jobs to Be Done Playbook* is a good starting point from a practical perspective, and for a high-level view, read Christensen's *Competing Against Luck*. For the full academic treatment, see *Acting with Technology* by Bonnie Nardi and Victor Kaptelinin.

If you are looking to do deeper reading, I would suggest reading *Badass* first then *The Jobs to Be Done Playbook*.

---

[8]
FUNCTIONAL, SOCIAL, AND EMOTIONAL

A process—whether it's buying a car, complying with regulators, or making coffee—has more than functional elements. There are social complexities (What other decision-makers are involved?) and emotional elements (How does completing the steps of the process make them feel?). There is an ecosystem of dimensions that work together to determine the kind of solution someone might consider.

The scripts in this book will help you probe the three different dimensions a problem can have. Understanding these motivations and constraints are critical to understanding why someone might choose, continue using, or discontinue using a product:

- A functional purpose
- An emotional dimension
- A social dimension

To continue the coffee example, someone may grind coffee beans because they want to use a specific grind texture (*functional*), they feel the work they put into it results in more enjoyable coffee (*emotional*), and they like sharing it with coworkers (*social*). Another person may choose pre-ground coffee in a pod because they're stressed in the morning (*emotional*), and they have to make their kids breakfast at the same time (*social*), which leads them to want the coffee-making process to be as simple as possible (*functional*). Even though both of those people are accomplishing the same goal ("be energized at work"), they have different combinations of functional, emotional, and social contexts that lead to different underlying processes and tool choices. Interviews will help you discover those underlying processes and purposes, and in turn, make products that better satisfy the different dimensions.

This even applies to luxury products. When someone buys a designer watch, they may tell themselves it's because of the lifetime guarantee and craftsmanship (*functional*), yet they may also be looking to impress others (*social*) and feel like they deserve it given their hard work (*emotional*).

Discovering motivations is not enough for a successful product, though. Toward that end, you'll also learn how to probe the commercial viability of those problems to understand where you might focus and how you might price by asking about:

- How often they experience it
- What they're currently paying to solve it
- How long it takes them

For example, someone who only makes coffee once a week for guests may buy a fancy pour-over set to impress their guests; they are in a relaxed setting and not pressed for time. A deadline-pressed journalist, on the other hand, who drinks multiple cups of coffee per day may prefer a pod machine as it is quick and efficient.

The same person who makes leisurely pour-over on the weekend may choose pods during the week when they are pressed for time.

Context, preferences, and constraints matter.

[9]
VALUABLE, USABLE, VIABLE, AND FEASIBLE

Listening to customers does not mean you literally do whatever they say.

(Just like how using empathy does not mean that you agree with everything that is being said.)

Everything you hear needs to be evaluated. According to product expert Marty Cagan, in order for a product to be successful, it needs to be valuable for the customer, usable by the customer, viable for the company to support commercially, and feasible for the company to build.[1]

- **Valuable**: If the product isn't something the customer needs, they won't buy it.
- **Usable**: If the customer can't figure out how to use it, they won't use it (even if the value is there).
- **Viable**: If it doesn't make money, the company will shut it down.
- **Feasible**: If it isn't possible for the company to build, it will never get off the ground.

A customer can't possibly know what your full capabilities, resources, incentives, and constraints are. After you finish interviewing someone, you will always need to filter what people say through those lenses of viability and feasibility. It may turn out that an idea a customer expresses is valuable, but different solutions to that problem need to be explored to find a solution that is usable, viable, and feasible.

Consider motorized personal transportation. The Segway is widely regarded as a product in search of a problem that never quite found its fit. But if you pull it back to the problem— "transport me in a way that's faster than walking without getting sweaty"—scooters also solve the same problem. Yet they have a different business model (*viability*) and form factors (*usability*) that better suit customer needs.

Crucially, this evaluation happens *after* the interview. During the interview, you should imagine yourself as a sponge that is there to absorb whatever the person says. Later, you can evaluate what might be a compelling opportunity. (We'll get into that more in Part VIII, "Analyzing Interviews.")

See Marty Cagan's *Inspired* for more on viable, valuable, usable, and feasible.

[PART 3]
GETTING STARTED

It can be bewildering to know where to start with interviewing, even if you're excited by what you might learn.

This section is your guide to becoming a confident and capable interviewer:

- You—yes, you—can do this
- Learn how to interview: a step-by-step guide
- Practice interviewing—no customers required!
- Practice interview script

[10]

YOU—YES YOU—CAN DO THIS

It's okay to question where you'll find the time to talk to people, and if you do, whether you'll get anything useful out of the experience.

It's okay to be afraid that it will be awkward.

It's okay to be nervous about whether you'll ask the right questions or afraid that you'll accidentally offend someone.

It's okay to have hesitations.

It's okay to make mistakes.

I've done thousands of interviews and still find myself making mistakes. It's okay. It is human to make mistakes; what matters is that you are conscious of them.

I encourage you to be gentle with yourself. Allow yourself to make mistakes and learn from them. According to Brené Brown, "the pressure to 'get it right' or 'say the perfect thing' can be the biggest barrier to empathy and compassion," and it is important to practice empathy with yourself and give yourself time and grace to learn this new skill.

(Or maybe you're brimming with excitement and can't wait to get started.)

No matter your starting point, this section is intended to serve as your roadmap to help you become a confident, effective interviewer. Your first interview may feel weird. Your second may feel weird. But by the tenth, you'll probably start getting the hang of it... and by your twentieth you might be able to think of the questions without referencing your script.

You may find it helpful to listen to the sample customer interview before, after, or while you read this book.

I recorded a sample interview as an episode of my podcast *Software Social*, and I encourage you to use it as a companion to this book. You will find a transcript of the interview in Part IX, Pulling It All Together: Sample Interview and Analysis and snippets of it throughout the book for illustration.

You can find it here: deployempathy.com/sample-interview.

Take it from another reader:

"Listening to the sample interview first made the whole process feel attainable. I listened to it while making and eating breakfast. I could hear Michele do what she talked about in the section on getting people to talk. The sample interview was key for me.

After, I did the practice interview with a former intern of mine. Both of us found the practice interview questions to flow very naturally, and I was surprised how easy it was to keep him talking about 90 percent of the time. At one point, I was afraid he'd share too much! I asked if he'd be open to interviewing me too, and he was, so we traded places. I almost learned more from being interviewed as I did being the interviewer myself.

Now I'm looking forward to finishing the book and interviewing real prospective customers." - *Nathan Pennington, software developer*

IT'S OKAY IF YOU'RE AFRAID YOU WON'T GET ANYTHING USEFUL OUT
OF TALKING TO CUSTOMERS

Oftentimes, the strongest objections to customer interviews come
from people who've tried them and didn't feel like they got anything
out of it.

When I dig into what happened to understand the broader context
behind that feeling, it often turns out they were ill-prepared, through
no fault of their own. Maybe they asked leading questions, or yes-or-
no questions. Maybe they didn't use a gentle tone of voice or they got
defensive when someone flagged an issue, which closed off the person
they were interviewing.

Or maybe they did the interviews for validation of an idea.

In the words of product designer Adam Amran, "validating" an
idea "smells of confirmation bias…[but] 'evaluating' would prime us to
be more open to new insights instead of looking to 'validate' what
we've assumed."[1]

This is something that teams at Stripe look out for, too. According
to Stripe product manager Theodora Chu, "it's important to take a
critical eye to make sure that you are using user research as an effective tool and not just using it as a way to say that you checked the box
of user research… if you were going to make a decision regardless [of
what users said], then you're wasting their time." And yours.

User interviews and research more broadly require an openness to
the idea that your idea may be wrong or incomplete. That idea may
feel threatening at first. It may take some time to switch your mindset
from being threatened by the idea of being wrong to being delighted
by and looking forward to it.

IT'S OKAY TO HAVE DOUBTS ABOUT WHETHER YOU CAN DO THIS

I want to step back for a moment and speak to you directly. Not to
you as a businessperson, but to you as a *person*, because the doubts
people have about whether they'll be able to learn interviewing often
speaks to deeper fears.

I've had people say to me that they would love to be able to do interviews themselves, but feel like their personality isn't suited to it.

Maybe it's because you feel uncomfortable asking questions and don't know what to say next. Perhaps you find it a challenge to come up with follow-up questions and are exhausted by the prospect of talking to people.

Or perhaps you often interrupt out of excitement and doubt whether you could suppress that instinct. Maybe you tend to get excited about what the other person is saying and want to jump in and relate your own experience or share your own ideas.

Regardless of your natural conversation style, this book can help you.

IT'S OKAY IF YOU FIND THE PROSPECT OF TALKING TO PEOPLE SCARY, DIFFICULT, AWKWARD, OR JUST PLAIN EXHAUSTING

If the idea of having conversations with people in general, never mind customers, freaks you out, that's okay.

Perhaps I should start with the good news about customer interviews for people who are a bit nervous about all of this: in a well-run interview, the interviewer only does ten percent of the talking.

In some ways, you'll have the opposite problem that people with more bubbly conversation styles, like me, have when learning to interview; rather than learning not to interrupt, you'll need to give yourself permission to take up space and dig deeper.

After reading that, one early reader of this book noted, "I have a fear of being annoying or burdensome by digging deeper." If that resonates, it's okay to be hesitant. Asking follow-up questions might grate against behaviors that have long protected you, and it may take a long time to become comfortable dropping those walls when acting as an interviewer.

You might find it easier to start with interactive interviews (such as testing a prototype or website) rather than digging into someone's process and emotions. The prototype, landing page, or whatever it is you are testing can act as a neutral third party in the interview and give you an easy way to deflect awkwardness.

When I've talked to people who identify as quiet who've read this book, it usually turns out that they're already using a lot of the skills in this book without consciously realizing it. For example, following up doesn't necessarily mean asking a question. It can also mean rephrasing what the person has said to elicit elaboration.

One developer founder/solo operator told me that they'd had five spoken conversations with customers in total over the four years they'd been running their software business. Reading this book made them realize they were already instinctively talking in a way that helps people open up, and all they needed were the specific questions to ask.

It may help to give yourself more time to practice with friends or family. Listening to the sample interview may also help calm some of your nerves around just how much you'll have to say.

You also may find interviewing more tiring. I generally recommend doing a maximum of two interviews per day, yet you may find that one per day or per week is more comfortable for you. I encourage you to find a method and approach that works for you.

It's okay to adapt the tools in this book to your own needs and comfort level. I hope you find that this book is for you as much as it is for people who already love talking to people.

IF YOU TEND TO EXCITEDLY OFFER YOUR OWN IDEAS

Perhaps your struggle is less with coming up with things to say and more with taking up too much airtime in the conversation.

Maybe you love sharing ideas when people present a problem. Or when they bring up something interesting at a dinner party, you share something interesting that is related, rather than digging deeper into what the person shared. These instincts come from a good place.

In some cases, "leadership potential" is communicated by sharing one's own ideas and being the loudest voice in the room. Talking is encouraged, rather than listening.

Validating how people feel is uncommon, too, even if you care about the person and the situation they're in. If someone is having a hard time, there is often an impulse to say something to the effect of "Things will get better!" or "At least [silver lining/worse thing didn't happen]," which is well-intended yet unfortunately dismissive. An empathetic response would have been "It sounds like you're having a hard time," which makes the person feel heard.

You probably learned your response patterns from those around you, and it's okay if you are just now thinking more deeply about those replies. If your instinct is to negate someone's tough experience as a way of making them feel better, it doesn't mean anything negative about you. It simply means that speaking empathetically was not part of your environment when you learned how to have conversations. Empathy is a learnable skill and you are doing the work to learn it by reading this book. The mere fact that you are currently reading a book about empathy shows that you care about other people.

If the tactics presented in this book seem very far from your normal conversation style, it's okay.

A male reader of an early version of this book mentioned as an aside something that's stuck in my head since: "Male socialization is basically a decades-long training program in how not to be an empathetic listener."

It reminded me of the classic book *What Got You Here Won't Get You There*, a book that was written for managers and organizational development folks to recommend to twenty-somethings that basically says, "Hey, all of those skills that were encouraged in school? Correcting others, showing how much better you were than other students, defending your ideas, and proving they were better? Yeah, all of that's actually counterproductive in the business world. Sorry, please stop."

I know this because *I* was told to read that book.

I wrote this book from the perspective of someone who had to learn active listening the hard way.

I had to learn how to submerge myself in what someone is saying.

Not to interrupt.

To leave pauses.

To mirror.

I've had to learn how to show empathy, to myself and others.

To validate how someone else feels.

To build rapport through listening.

To let them find the answers, rather than sharing my own ideas.

I tell you all of this to say: if I learned how to do this, anyone can.

You can do this.

[11]
LEARN HOW TO INTERVIEW: A STEP-BY-STEP GUIDE

STEP 1: READ THE "HOW TO TALK SO PEOPLE WILL TALK" SECTION.

"How to Talk So People Will Talk" will teach you the conversational tactics to use in an interview to get someone to open up.

You may find it helpful to apply the tactics to everyday conversations for practice. These tactics can be used with coworkers, people you mentor, friends, and family members. Rather than being weirded out, the person you're talking to will probably think you've magically become an excellent listener overnight!

→ You'll know you learned something from that section if you find yourself noticing your own conversation tactics in everyday conversations. For example, if someone is telling you about something interesting that happened to them, if you notice an urge to relate your own experience rather than dive deeper into their experience. (It's okay if you find yourself still doing those things—you don't have to change your normal social conversation style. Being aware of it, and adjusting accordingly in interviews, is all you need to do.)

STEP 2: DO A PRACTICE INTERVIEW.

There is a practice interview, with a script, topic, and instructions for finding someone to interview, in the next chapter. The practice interview can be done with a friend or family member and has a very broad topic that anyone should be able to speak to (the most recent purchase they made).

Record the interview (with the interviewee's permission).

If you can, try to get the other person to switch places and interview *you*. You may very well learn just as much from being interviewed yourself as you do from being the interviewer.

→ You'll know you're learning when you notice if the other person goes against the "How to Talk So People Will Talk" tactics and how that impacts your own sharing when being interviewed yourself.

STEP 3: ANALYZE THE PRACTICE INTERVIEW FOR WHAT YOU LEARNED *AND* HOW YOU CONDUCTED IT.

After the interview, listen back to the recording and analyze it from two different angles: first, the information you gathered, and second, how you conducted the interview.

Try to get a rough sense for the different functional/emotional/social factors that went into their decision, the overall goal they were trying to achieve by buying it, and some of the steps.

1. Answer the overall questions:

- What is their overall goal?
- What did they use before (including homemade/manual solutions)?
- How frequent is the problem they experienced?
- How difficult is it for them to solve that problem?
- What are the costs of getting it wrong?

2. Outline the steps of their decision-making process. (This may not be a linear process, and that's okay.)

3. Identify the different factors that went into their decision:

- Functional Factor(s)
- Emotional Factor(s)
- Social Factor(s)

→ You've done this right if you can identify the different factors and the steps of the process. It's okay if you don't find all of the steps.

Next, think about the different interview skills in "How to Talk So People Will Talk," and notice which of the skills you used naturally versus which ones might need more focus. It's okay (and expected) that many of the tactics do not come naturally to you.

If the person says something to the effect of, "Well, I didn't really think about it at the time..." or "I've never really thought about it, but..." that's an encouraging sign, because then you know you've dug beyond the conscious level and gotten them to open up. Great products not only solve the big problem but little steps that people didn't realize could be easier, and finding those "I never really thought about it..." moments is key.

STEP 4: INTERVIEW ONE PERSON, THEN A FEW MORE.

Once you've built an awareness of how you might need to adjust your conversation style for interviews and a sense for asking about a process and the underlying motivations, you're ready to start interviewing potential customers or customers.

It's okay if it takes you a few weeks or months to go from Step 3 to Step 4. I have a founder friend who saw me speak about customer interviewing in 2019 and it took her two years to get comfortable with the concept and start interviewing herself. (Now interviewing customers is her favorite part of her job.)

The "Recruiting Participants" section will help you find people to interview, even if you don't have any customers.

The "Scripts and Templates" section contains scripts for specific scenarios, like validating an idea, talking to a relatively new customer, or talking to a long-time customer.

Start with one person at first, see how it goes, and adjust your script or approach before doing another. You may find that you need to adjust your targeting or questions. Slowly work your way up to five interviews.

If you have a product with a churn problem, you may understandably want to start there. However, cancellation interviews are the most challenging interviews. I encourage you to become comfortable talking to existing customers first. They will also be happier to talk to you, and that positive feedback will give you momentum going into cancellation interviews.

It's okay if you find yourself forgetting questions or accidentally interrupting people. Record the interviews with permission, and then listen back to them. Pay attention to where you could have dug deeper or used a different tactic to help them open up more.

→ You'll know you did this right if you walk away from each interview saying, "Wow! I didn't realize that [...]" Success is walking away excited about what you've learned, with new questions to answer, and full of ideas for things you could do differently.

STEP 5: ANALYZE YOUR INTERVIEWS.

After you've interviewed five people, it's time to stop and analyze. The "Analyzing Interviews" chapter will give you specific tools for digesting and organizing what you've heard.

If you're doing discovery for a new product and feel like you've heard different things from each person, that's okay. It simply means you have a broad scope and have an opportunity to narrow down the scope. The analysis tools in that chapter will help you do just that.

→ You'll know you're doing the analysis right if you can identify the overall goal someone is trying to achieve, diagram the steps that go into that process, and identify where the relevant problem fits. You'll know you've really got the hang of it when you're able to identify different functional, emotional, and social components and are able to identify the frequency and time and money spent for relevant steps.

STEP 6: MAKE INTERVIEWING A REGULAR PART OF YOUR PROCESS.

Interviewing shouldn't put the rest of your work on hold.

Interviewing should be integrated into your process, whether it's because you have a specific problem to solve (like which features to prioritize, how to stop churn, or what to build) or as part of your everyday workflow to continually update your customer understanding.

Depending on how well understood a problem is, you may need to do further "research loops" to narrow the scope of a problem. For a complex problem or the discovery stage, that is almost expected. (See more in Chapter 17, "Research Loops.")

Even if you only do one interview a month, you'll be gathering more understanding and ideas than before.

[12]
PRACTICE INTERVIEWING—NO CUSTOMERS NEEDED!

It's okay if the prospect that an interview may be a waste of time deters you from even trying.

Perhaps you've tried asking people whether they would buy what you've made or what they think of something before, and you didn't really get much out of it.

The job of this book is to give you tried-and-true questions and help you ask them in a way that gives you actionable information.

The worst thing that can happen is that the person on the other end finds it awkward and you feel like you've wasted fifteen minutes.

And that's it!

Of the thousands of interviews I've conducted, I can think of only a handful where I didn't learn anything. (And sometimes, *not* learning something is helpful in its own right because you're getting validation.)

It's okay to have nerves about this.

I think if we were to sit down with that nervousness and listen to it—and not challenge it, or try to overcome it, or act like it doesn't exist—and gently ask it what it needs, I think it might ask for just a little bit of practice before you bring this out into the wider world.

What can be helpful is a nice, low-stakes environment to practice these skills and get a sense for just how this sort of, quite frankly, socially unusual situation plays out. A calm venue where you can learn how to dig for details and uncover a process without the risk that you're offending a customer.

The practice activity in this chapter will help you do just that.

And I know this practice activity will help you overcome the hill of getting started with interviews, because I've seen it with my own eyes.

About four years ago, some friends and I started a Meetup group for people interested in the product development/marketing/research framework Jobs to Be Done for the Washington, DC area. Most of the people who joined the group were research-curious and not practitioners themselves yet. People were excited about doing interviews and how it could reshape how they thought about their products and customers, yet there was some uncertainty about how to actually do an interview.

So, we decided to do an interview workshop. We paired people up and had them practice interviewing one another.

I was paired with a woman named Rachel, a product analyst with a quantitative data analysis background. I remember her being a little nervous and tentative about interviews.

We followed the script below, with a similar prompt: "What's something new you bought in the last three months?" The idea was to ask about a purchase we'd made that was new to us and understand why we switched.

The product that I said I'd bought recently was a bottle of shampoo: Suave Professionals Sea Minerals Shampoo, to be exact.

When I bought it, I hadn't really thought much about the purchase. It was on sale, and I saw it on the end cap as I was going through the grocery store and grabbed it.

Simple, right?

Well, what Rachel was able to discover—which impresses me to this day—was that it was much more than something I happened to grab as I walked by in the store. Why had I picked that one, even though there were many other varieties also part of that same sale on that same shelf?

Through the script, she was able to uncover why that particular item had jumped at me among a sea of other options on that shelf. I'd gone to the beach a few weeks beforehand with friends, and thought my hair looked good that week, and wondered whether it was the salt in the water that helped my hair look good. I have, and had, no idea if that was true, but I was willing to try. She was able to find my hope for the product (make me look as good as I did at the beach) and what the original problem was I was trying to solve (my hair is very thin, and getting more volume into it is a constant struggle). The thought of my voluminous beach hair—and the feeling of being at the beach, wind in my hair, good friends around me—is what led me to take a chance on that particular bottle of shampoo.

And Rachel was able to find all of that underlying emotion and memory even as a first-time interviewer, with about the same amount of training on qualitative customer research that you've received by reading this book to this point.

We then switched, and I interviewed Rachel about her own recent purchase. In her case, it was a phone subscription, and we talked about why she'd switched (to get more data so she could watch Netflix on the bus to work) and whether it was working as she'd hoped.

It was almost magical to see the gears turning in her head. Interviewing and being interviewed herself helped her see not only how to do the interview but the kind of insights they unlock that lurk below the surface.

Rachel was able to take the confidence from that workshop and start interviewing real customers to augment the quantitative data she was already analyzing. She continued doing so, and went on to become a first product manager and then a senior product manager.

I would see her every so often for a few years after—she worked with my husband—and every time I saw her, somehow, the shampoo would come up, and she'd then excitedly tell me about interviews she'd had recently and what she'd learned. Interviewing went from scary and unknown to exciting and full of discovery.

[13]

PRACTICE INTERVIEW SCRIPT

A good partner for this is someone you're loosely connected to or a stranger. Think: someone you tweet with occasionally but don't know in real life, a coworker in a different department, a friend's roommate, or your partner's friend.

Someone you know vaguely and not too closely.

A close friend or family member is not a good candidate, as you probably have somewhat of an understanding of their psychology and purchasing habits. And they may be wary of sharing too much.

For this practice, you'll use the Customer/Problem Discovery Script to understand why they tried a new product. You're going to ask them about something they bought that was new to them. The key is that it should be something a) they purchased themselves and b) is a new purchase (i.e., not a specific item they buy regularly. A new-to-them-but-used item is fine). It might be an item they've bought before but a different brand, or a category of product they've never bought before.

After you interview them, I strongly encourage you to switch places and let them interview *you*. You may learn just as much if not more from being interviewed yourself.

For this, you will need:

- A script (below)
- Someone to interview
- Fifteen to twenty minutes
- A way to record the interview

What you want to listen for is:

- What is the underlying problem/need this product solved for them?
- How often do they experience the problem?
- Were they previously paying to solve that problem? What did they use?
- How much time does this problem take for them?
- How important is the problem for them? If they don't solve it, or it's solved poorly, what are the consequences?
- Who else was involved in the decision?

And you want to probe the following dimensions of the problem and decision process:

- Functional (i.e., the literal problem the product solves)
- Emotional (how they will feel if the problem is/is not solved, and how they feel about the new solution)
- Social (whether they talked to others about the purchase before or after, whether there were any social implications of how the problem was solved)

PRACTICE INTERVIEW QUESTIONS

Note: The questions are not grammatically perfect, and that is on purpose to put the other person at ease.

1. Thank you for taking the time to talk to me. I recognize this may be a little strange, but this will help me with [work/side project/etc.]. Is it okay if I record this?
2. To start, can you tell me about a product you bought for the first time recently?
3. Where were you when you bought it?
4. Were you with anyone else when you bought it?
5. How did you make the purchase?
6. Before you bought it, was there anything about it that was kind of an open question about it to you?
7. Where did you first learn about the product?
8. What did you do when you first came across [the product]?
9. Did you talk to anyone else before you made the purchase?
10. What were you hoping [the product] would do for you?
11. What other products did you try before this?
12. How did it go when you first used it?
13. Can you tell me about whether it did what you were hoping it would do?
14. Would you buy [this product] again?

[PART 4]
WHEN SHOULD YOU DO INTERVIEWS?

This section presents a mental model for thinking about two different types of research. You'll find this model both at my company Geocodio and at Stripe.

Project-based research is helpful for answering specific questions, like "why do people keep asking support about [this]?"

Ongoing research is helpful to building out a general bank of customer understanding and informing broader decision-making.

Each company needs to find their own research flow, so I present this less as a canonical example of what your customer research pipeline should be, and more as a jumping off point for you to think about how you could integrate it into your own work.

[14]
INTERVIEWS OR NUMBERS?

Before we get into the mental model for knowing when to interview, let's discuss a common question.

People sometimes ask me whether they should talk to customers instead of looking at analytics.

My answer is simple: do both!

Quantitative and qualitative research are not an either/or and instead should be used together as part of a broader effort to understand the business and the customers that fuel it.

If you want metrics to move, you need to find the context and the story behind them. Interviewing customers can give you that context.

Only people can tell you why they bought a product or took certain actions and didn't take others.

And similarly, an interview will never tell you how many people are doing something.

Do both.

Or perhaps, "do all."

Looking at data is one tool in your toolbox, surveys are another, and interviews yet another (of many different research tools in that toolbox).

This book focuses on interviewing since there are so few resources written about it in depth that are accessible to people who do not come from a user experience perspective.

For more on different types of qualitative and quantitative research and when to use them, see Erika Hall's *Just Enough Research*.

SELECTING THE RIGHT TOOL FOR THE JOB AT STRIPE

At Stripe, user interviews are regarded as a tool to solve a problem, and though they are "a tool that we tend to use probably more so than the average company," in the words of Stripe product manager Theodora Chu.[1] User interviews are used in combination with other types of research, like industry research and data analysis.

Their process looks like this:

1. Align on a problem to solve.

2. Determine whether user interviews are the right way to solve it and what other data might be needed.

3. If user interviews are the right tool for the job, make sure the questions they're asking will solve the problem they've set out to solve.

You'll read more about Stripe's research process in the next few pages.

[15]
PROJECT-BASED RESEARCH

Project-based research has a narrowly defined question, a defined goal, and a defined timeline.

For example, you may be curious about an observation, like:

- "Why aren't more people buying this product from this landing page?"
- "How could we reduce the number of customer support tickets we receive about [X]?"
- "Should we launch a new product [for a given problem?]"
- "What else might people want from this prototype before we make it a real product?"

I'll walk you through how this usually looks for us with Geocodio.

Usually a project-based effort will involve a combination of quantitative and qualitative research. A question will emerge, and we'll look for related data we might already have on hand. Usually that means a combination of diving into our analytics to get a numerical perspective first, and looking through customer support history. Depending on the problem, it may also involve surveys and competitor research.

Once we have a quantitative picture and have confidence that this problem is at enough of a scale and business impact to warrant investigation, we then set up interviews. These might be phone calls or screen shares with five to ten customers over the course of two weeks. Afterward, we brainstorm and perhaps wireframe or prototype solutions, go back to those same customers and ask them for further feedback, and so forth. The entire process might take one to two months, and is run concurrently with other work.

This process works for us as a two-person team, yet it's also the kind of process that can work at a larger company.

TARGETED RESEARCH AT STRIPE

Talking to users is so baked into the culture and core of Stripe that they don't have one formal codified process for research. Teams might keep a pulse on user needs through ongoing research (covered in Chapter 18), and shift into exploring a specific problem once they notice patterns. According to Stripe product manager Theodora Chu, "targeted research comes out of a problem we've been getting a lot of feedback on, or when we're seeing a rising need for something."[1]

Here is how you might see a team at Stripe approach targeted research:

1. Write out the specific problem hypothesis or question they want answered,
2. Kickoff with all relevant stakeholders (engineering, design, product, marketing, sales, or pricing), plus a dedicated user researcher if available
3. Define the characteristics of users that would help them confirm or deny that problem hypothesis,
4. Brainstorm a list of all questions that would help them answer the problem,
5. Curate questions by removing duplicates and leading questions,
6. Workshop the questions internally for flow and relevancy,

7. Pull a list of users (either current customers or prospects and customers of competitor products),
8. Reach out to targeted users,[2] and
9. Interview users.

What's truly remarkable about Stripe's approach is that it isn't just user researchers who interview users. According to Chu, the work-shopping process results in a script that "almost anyone can run with and go talk to users and get high-quality signal."[3]

Stripe's process is unusually decentralized and streamlined for a large company.

The more internal stakeholders, the longer and more complex a process will be. It will vary from company to company and situation to situation. Yet the fundamentals are the same: identify a question, get a sense for the size and value of the problem, talk to people, iterate, and repeat.

If you would like an introduction to research approaches at larger companies, I suggest the second half of Jim Kalbach's *The Jobs to Be Done Playbook*. For those in design agencies, see Erika Hall's *Just Enough Research*.

---

[16]

HOW MANY PEOPLE SHOULD YOU TALK TO?

For any discrete problem, the general rule is to to find five people to talk to before making decisions.

(That decision may be to build or change something, but it may also be to do more qualitative or quantitative research.)

The seminal "Voice of the Customer" paper by Abbie Griffin and John Hauser in 1993 found that twenty to thirty people were needed to surface 90 to 95 percent of customer needs and twelve people to surface 80 percent.[1] User researchers Tom Landauer and Jakob Nielsen of Nielsen Norman Group have found that 80 percent of needs can be surfaced by five interviews.[2]

While both of these analyses were in the context of usability studies, I have generally found them to be true for qualitative interviews. For most questions, five interviews is enough to get going. For complex problems, ten to fifteen may be necessary.

(I interviewed thirty readers of early drafts of this book, but admittedly, I just love talking to people about talking to people.)

Jim Kalbach in *The Jobs to Be Done Playbook* also recommends talking to a minimum of five people and a maximum of fifteen to twenty. I usually aim for five people, though the real rule is "Stop when you start hearing the same things over and over again."

Before making decisions, you should also have some supporting research, like analytics, competitor research, or other data. (See Erika Hall's *Just Enough Research* for more on other kinds of research.)

Your decision after those five people may be that you need to narrow the scope, do additional kinds of research, and talk to another five people on a specific branch of the problem you're exploring. That's okay. It doesn't mean you're doing something wrong if you don't feel like you have a definitive path after five interviews.

PARTICIPANT DIVERSITY

It's important to speak to a diverse group of customers or potential customers, both for ethical reasons and for business opportunity reasons.

While you only have so much control over who replies to your emails, posts, and other recruitment efforts, the more diverse your research participants, the more complete your research will be, and the clearer idea you'll have of different opportunities.

Derek Featherstone is an accessibility consultant who has phrased the importance of incorporating people with disabilities specifically into research:[3]

"Conducting research to uncover pain points using your product? Include disabled people. You'll find two things:

1. Some people with disabilities experience the same pain points as people without.
2. Pain points emerge that you weren't aware of because you hadn't included people with disabilities before.

For example, your research showed that people consume podcasts on the go, most often using their mobile device.

But the research didn't include people with disabilities... so it didn't show that people who are Deaf or hard-of-hearing prefer to consume on their computer where transcripts are easier to consume (either on their own or with audio)."

Leaving out groups of users therefore means leaving opportunities on the table.

If you'd like an introduction to accessibility, consider *Accessibility for Everyone* by Lara Kalbag. *Mismatch: How Inclusion Shapes Design* by Kat Holmes discusses how inclusion can be a source of innovation.

---

[17]

RESEARCH LOOPS

If you hear completely different processes and tools on each call with limited overlap, it's okay. It simply means you have a broad research scope.

In early exploratory stages, you might consider doing research loops: talk to five people, analyze what you hear, and see which problems seem directionally interesting to you (nexus of what you're able to build and seems commercially viable), and then conduct interviews with another group of five, whittle down again, another group of five, and so forth.

First, find an initial group of five people to talk to, then analyze the problems you hear:

- Frequent and painful problems
- Underserved problems (e.g., people are doing things manually)
- Commercially viable problems (people already pay for a solution)
- Problems that lead to solutions that are feasible for you or your organization to create

At this point, you might narrow it down to one to three different problem areas to continue exploring—either through prototyping followed by interactive interviews, or further interviews, depending on how well you think you understand the problem from the customer's perspective.

You might then continue to narrow down what a solution might look like via card sorting interviews and interactive interviews with prototypes or wireframes.

[18]

ONGOING RESEARCH

If project-based research is a remodel, ongoing research is rearranging the furniture and organizing the shelves.

It's also the research that, over time, can lead to completely relocating or rebuilding the house. (If you want.)

Ongoing research is research that you do every day as part of adding to your ever-expanding and evolving understanding of customer needs.

For us, there are two primary ways we do ongoing research: short surveys with a follow-up question, and interviews with new, happy, and canceled customers.

But first, let's talk about ongoing research at Stripe.

ONGOING RESEARCH AT STRIPE

At Stripe, teams might conduct both targeted research about specific questions and broad-based research to "get a gut check about how people are feeling about the product," according to Stripe product manager Theodora Chu.

Every few months, Chu's team at Stripe sends out an email to users who have recently onboarded or have taken certain actions the team is interested in. This email looks like:

"Hey, we saw you just did [X]. If you're open to it, we'd love to hop on a call and learn more about what went well, what didn't, and how we can do better."

Even though not all users reply, it still allows the team to check the pulse of users. All team members, including developers and product managers, participate on the calls. This ongoing research can then feed into targeted research as the team notices themes over time. This combination of targeted and ongoing research helps teams answer the key question at Stripe: "who are the users and what do they care about?"

If you're in a team, the inclusion of as many team members from different functions is critical for alignment.

As Erika Hall notes in *Just Enough Research*, "People who have a hand in collecting insights will look for opportunities to apply them. Being one of the smart people is more fun than obeying the smart person, which is how the researcher/designer dynamic can feel if designers are merely the recipients of the analysis."[1]

I've seen this dynamic first-hand myself, and also the sea change in motivation and alignment that can happen once the whole team is included in the research process.

SHORT SURVEYS WITH A FOLLOW-UP QUESTION

People often picture surveys as something with multiple questions, yet I've found the shorter the survey, the higher the response rate.

A one-question survey is still a survey, and you can still get valuable information with just one open-ended question.

(An automated email with just one calibrated open-ended question can technically be a survey!)

You just need to ask the right question.

On an everyday basis, I suggest running short, one- or two-question surveys that are integrated into the product experience.

Longer surveys are an important part of customer research and since they're well-covered elsewhere, they aren't covered in this book. For more on survey design, see Erika Hall's *Just Enough Research*.

We've run short surveys on our user dashboard for five years now. We use a simple corner box survey with two questions: a one through ten satisfaction rating and an open-ended question. We're checking to make sure we're getting mostly nines and tens, and ask for details from anyone who gives us below a seven, as that may indicate something went wrong.

Usually Net Promoter Score tools are well-suited to this. We use SatisMeter and can also recommend Thermostat.io. Net Promoter Score itself is somewhat problematic (both in theory and in how they are used), but I believe that the general one through ten score is helpful as a pulse check, and the built-in ability for a quick follow-up question is a helpful springboard to deeper questions and conversations.

For a long time, the open-ended question was, "What could we do better?" ... but we didn't really get a lot of actionable feedback.

I realized that was because we were basically asking our customers to do our work for us.

More than 80 percent of customers left the field blank.

Garbage question, garbage back.

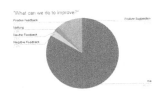

So we pivoted to using them for high-value, easy to answer questions.

One of the crucial parts of Jobs to Be Done interviews is figuring out how someone overcame the inertia of their existing solution and switched to something new.

Asking people what they used before is also a relatively straight-forward question to answer.

Note that asking "What did you use before you used [product]?" is a simpler question than "Why did you switch to [product]?". "What did you use…" is factual, while "Why did you switch?" asks for emotions and thoughts and decision-making and causality, which may not be clear-cut.

Interestingly, asking the factual question can make it easier to pull out the decision process precisely because it isn't part of the question.

When we changed it to, "What did you use before you found Geocodio?" this is what the answers looked like:

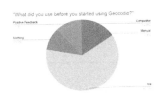

We then reply to the open-ended replies and will often include an ask to set up a call. (You can see examples of those templates in Chapter 24, "Surveys.")

Some questions to consider using in a one-question survey that are both easy to answer and highly insightful include:

- *What did you use before you used [product]?*
- *How did you come across [product]?*

I don't suggest using the magic wand question ("If you could change anything about [product] with a magic wand, what would it be?") here, as you'll likely get a lot of responses from people wanting it to cost less or be free, and that wouldn't be entirely useful to you.

NEW CUSTOMERS

It takes a lot of energy to switch from one product to another. There are different factors that simultaneously inspire someone to make a change and also stay where they are.

In the Jobs to Be Done world, this is known as the "Four Forces." It is a way of diagramming the external forces that push someone towards a new solution, internal forces that pull them towards it, as well as the anxieties and inertia that cause them to stay put. See Alan Klement's *When Coffee and Kale Compete* for more.

By uncovering that motivation, you can better understand and speak to the reasons that might lead others to switch. By speaking to those reasons, you can gain more new customers.

New customer interviews are particularly helpful for finding marketing ideas, as people may be seeking out your product for reasons you didn't realize. Whenever I talk to new customers, I often find myself in a flurry of writing landing pages in the days after.

Landing pages themselves can be a part of your research process. For example, over the years we've heard here and there about people using Geocodio for distance calculations. I finally sat down and wrote a landing page about how to do that in Excel a few months ago. It's now our top-performing landing page, and as I write this book, we're exploring what a *usable* interface might look like and how to make it *viable* from a business perspective. (Pulling in the Marty Cagan framework, *feasibility* and *value* have already been determined.)

I suggest doing these interviews with people who have started using your product or service within the last one to three months. I find that if you do it too soon (say, within a week or two of signing up), people tend to think it's an onboarding call and will have questions about getting set up. Onboarding calls make sense in a lot of contexts, but are a separate conversation from this interview. The goal here is to talk to people who have already started using the service and are successfully set up so you can dig a level deeper into why they started using it.

HAPPY CUSTOMERS AND CANCELED CUSTOMERS

People generally quickly see the value of talking to customers who've canceled. But the one that seems to surprise other people the most is intentionally interviewing long-time happy customers. Talking to happy customers who pay every month without complaint is sometimes a mental leap.

Talking to people who've canceled seems intuitive to most people since you want to know how you can get them back or prevent more people from canceling. But interviewing people who are happily renewing every month or year? Most companies never talk to their happiest customers outside of customer support and sales settings. Yet, they are precisely the people with use cases that are well-served by your product. Sometimes people are afraid to poke the bear and ask them why they are happy, but most of the time, the unhappy customers are much louder and take up the air in the room.

Spending more time on people who cancel than those who stay is a symptom of loss aversion. Loss aversion is a concept pioneered by

Daniel Kahneman and Amos Tversky, and it's the phenomenon that people would rather avoid losing money than gaining the same amount.[2] In this sense, loss aversion means spending more time trying to stop people from canceling (or win them back) rather than spending time on existing satisfied customers and trying to find more people with similar use cases.

In short, loss aversion is that pernicious voice that makes you pay more attention to people who are upset rather than those who are happy. It is a normal human instinct, and it's okay if you notice that you do this.

Fixing bugs is one thing, but changing your product to better fit someone's use case that it wasn't designed for is another. Focusing on the happy people—i.e., the people whose use case *is* a good match for what your product already does, or is in scope for your company—is much easier and more enjoyable. The more you can balance the scales between happy and canceled customer interviews, the better, because acting on the feedback, problems, and insights from happy customers will tilt the balance toward use cases that are well-served by your product. The more happy customer interviews you do, the fewer cancelation ones you'll need to do, because there will simply be fewer people canceling. In this way, happy customer interviews are almost like preemptive cancelation interviews because they will lead you to get rid of things that attract people who aren't a good fit.

To see which customers are likely to be in your "happy customer" category, look at your revenue data and try to talk to a representative sample of the customers who make up your top 80 percent of revenue. It can help you evaluate whether customer segments and patterns you think exist do exist and how you could improve your business (whether from a marketing or product development perspective) to better serve the use cases that are the best fit for your product. The worst-case scenario is that these high-value customers feel honored that you've spent the time to talk to them, and turn into an advocate for your product.

Feel free to mix and match quantitative and qualitative analysis tools to make them fit your needs and the unique circumstances of your business. Interviewing should be only one tool in your toolbox. We do other kinds of research, like using landing pages as a way to gauge interest in a potential new feature, creating longer surveys, and performing keyword analysis.

For more on other kinds of research, see Erika Hall's *Just Enough Research*.

[PART 5]
RECRUITING PARTICIPANTS

Once you've got the techniques down and know what you want to figure out, you still need to find people to talk to you.

Thankfully, because of social media, this is much easier than it might have been fifteen or certainly thirty years ago.

I break out recruiting users into two categories here: social media and forums (for non-customers) and email and surveys (for current and former customers).

This part includes templates for recruiting in several different places:

- Reddit and forums
- Twitter
- LinkedIn
- Facebook groups and email lists
- Email
- Surveys

[19]

REDDIT AND FORUMS

You're aware you should evaluate your ideas with people and that it's better to spend five hours and fifty dollars on gift cards for a handful of user interviews than building something for months and have it launch to crickets.

Yet what if you're building something new and don't have any users to talk to? How exactly do you find people to talk to?

Where?

Reddit (and other niche forums).

This section assumes you have already found relevant niche communities. For guidance on that step, see Amy Hoy and Alex Hillman's online course *Sales Safari*.

This section will help you take it to the next level and find people to talk to you.

Here is what you'll need:

- A list of niche-relevant subreddits to post to
- Copy for a recruitment post
- An interview script
- Approximately five to ten hours (Up to five hours for interviews, plus five hours for planning/follow-up)
- [Optional: a budget equivalent to $50]

Depending on who you're looking to talk to, a budget for incentives may be helpful. A phone call may not require an incentive, but a screen share test usually does since it feels more like work to the other person.

Step 1: Determine who you want to talk to, and who you don't.

The more specific you can be, the better. Let's say you have a calendar scheduling app. Do you want to talk to administrative assistants, solo founders, business coaches, consultants, doctors, etc.? Pick one audience to start.

Step 2: Research subreddits for that topic.

There are subreddits for *everything*, even professional fields—something that often takes people by surprise. (Reddit is not all cat pictures and betting on stocks.)

For a project I did a few years ago, I needed to talk to data developers in the healthcare industry. Turns out there is a subreddit devoted to HealthIT with five thousand members. Score!

Step 3: Check that the post you're about to make is allowed by that subreddit or forum.

Some subreddits may forbid this. Even if it isn't explicitly forbidden, your post will want to tread lightly. Extinguish any urge to use this as a sales or marketing opportunity, and definitely avoid any promotional language.

Step 4: Write your post.

I suggest creating a new Reddit username for this to keep everything organized.

Go for a casual tone of voice. The points you want to hit on are:

- You're looking for people to help you for research
- Describe the problem you're looking to understand, without giving away too much detail so as not to bias them toward your solution to the problem
- Who you are looking to talk to
- What people will be expected to do
- How they can contact you if interested
- [Optional: The incentive they'll receive if they participate]

Try to keep each point to a sentence each, and use line breaks between sentences to increase scannability.

For our calendaring app, this post might look like:

Subreddit: r/VirtualAssistant

Looking for people to talk to about the complexities of scheduling meetings—$10 Amazon gift card if you participate!

I'm looking to talk to virtual assistants about the process they go through to schedule meetings.

I'm a software developer and I'm looking to create a product that would reduce the complexity of scheduling meetings, and I want to better understand people's current processes.

It would be a thirty-minute phone call and I'm looking for five people to talk to sometime in the next two weeks.

All calls will be kept confidential.

If interested, please DM me a little bit about your work background and how I can get in touch with you.

Thanks!

Here's an example from software consultant Nate Bosscher:

Step 5: Sort through applicants.

You may decide to post to one subreddit, or cross-post to multiple if you're only able to find small communities.

Remember that HealthIT subreddit I mentioned with five thousand members? It's not a particularly large subreddit, but I still got roughly seventy replies back. But you don't need to talk to that many people!

It may sound like a lot, yet the time you spend researching will be much less than the time you might spend building something that ends up being the wrong product.

From that seventy, I whittled it down to people who best fit who I needed to talk to, and set up calls with them. A few people might not get back to you, so I would try to set up calls with seven to eight people to start. This might look something like:

Hey, thanks for your interest in talking to me about meeting scheduling! I'd love to hear about your experiences. I'm available on Mondays from 3–6pm Eastern,Wednesdays from 8–10pm, and Saturdays from 11–1—what would work best for you for a half-hour call?

Make sure to include a weekend window, an after-work window, and a workday window. I've rarely had weekend calls, but some people may not be able to swing it during the work day.

For people you don't select, make sure you message them back acknowledging their message. This might look something like:

Hey, thanks for your interest in talking to me about meeting scheduling. I already have the number of participants I need, but if someone falls through I'll let you know!

Once you have the calls scheduled, comment on your post that you have enough people for now so people who come across the post in a few days/months/years know you're all set.

Step 6: Conduct the calls.

If you're doing problem exploration, use the customer/problem discovery script.

If you have something they can interact with (a landing page, a prototype, a wireframe), use the interactive interview script.

Step 7: Send the gift card while you're on the phone at the end.

This person doesn't know you and is talking to you to be helpful, but also for the incentive. Trust is tenuous. I would suggest closing the call by saying, "Okay, to wrap up, I'm going to send you the gift card now via Amazon. Can you confirm when you receive it?" and wait for them to confirm.

It's also worth considering asking them to post a comment that the interview was legitimate.

Why is this so important? Because you might need to come back to this sub for more research later, and you want to leave a good impression—even if it's all anonymous. If you don't send it promptly, people will post. You want to end up with a comment like:

Just FYI, I talked to this person yesterday. They were super nice and it wasn't a sales pitch, and I got the gift card. Not a scam!

rather than

They never sent me my gift card! BEWARE!

If a call goes well, you can ask people to make a post confirming that it went well and was legitimate:

Hey, any chance you'd consider making a comment on that post, just so other people know this is legit and not a scam?

Step 8: Send them a follow-up thank-you note within the next day.

It's important to also write a personal thank-you—even after you've thanked them on the call and sent them the gift card. This might look something like:

Hi,

I just wanted to thank you again for taking the time to talk to me yesterday about [topic]. It was helpful to hear about the different steps you go through and all of the tools you use for this, and the different challenges that come up. I learned a lot from you.

Thanks again,

Your name

[20]
TWITTER

Twitter is a great way to build problem-space understanding by finding people who are already talking about what you might be trying to do—both the problem itself and how well your competitors solve it.

Amy Hoy and Alex Hillman's *Sales Safari* course teaches people how to find digital watering holes where their potential customers are already talking about their problems and their opinions of competitors.[1] Their approach is called "internet ethnography," and many of the *Sales Safari* tactics have become best practices. [2]

Here, I will assume that you've already found those digital watering holes and done some foundational research on the problem space and customer base. This chapter focuses on how you can get people to talk to you to get further details that they may not have posted about. On Twitter, the key will be to find people who experience the problem and have already spoken about it. This may take the form of:

- They're negatively posting/tweeting about a competitor
- They're negatively posting/tweeting about the process

- They've blogged or posted links about the process and described going through relevant negative steps

Do as much research as you can on someone before reaching out. When you reach out, make sure to include evidence that you've done your research. For example, you can link to the tweet where they express having that problem, or a blog post they've written about it.

When you find someone who tweets about how a competitor product frustrates them in some way, you can reply or DM them. Be as friendly and nonintrusive as possible. Since DMing is more intrusive, try to do some research on them in advance. When else have they posted about this? What other information can you find about their experience to ask better questions?

REPLYING TO TWEETS ABOUT THE PROBLEM

If you don't have a product

Hey, I'm thinking about building something related to [thing you posted about]. I noticed you were unhappy with [competitor]. (Link to their post) Any chance you'd be willing to have a call with me about it?

You don't always have to have a call. (This is not getting you out of calls—but rather that they're not always necessary.)

Can you say more about how this frustrated you? (link to their post) I'm thinking of building something that solves this and am eager to learn about what people think of the options already out there.

If you have a prototype

Hey, I saw you [feeling] about [process/thing]. [link to their post] I'm building something to try to make this easier. Any chance you'd take a look at my prototype and give me your thoughts? I promise I'm not trying to sell you, just trying to get feedback.

If you have a product

Hey, I notice you're specifically frustrated with [X], and my [thing] aims to make that easier. [link to their post] Any chance you'd take a look at it and give me your thoughts? (I'm not trying to sell you, I promise, just want to get feedback.)

Via DM, you can be a bit more detailed:

Hey, I noticed you tweeted about [competitor/problem space/etc]. I'm looking to build something that solves that. Is there any chance you'd be willing to have a 15–20 minute call with me about it? If so, [here is my calendar link/scheduling info]

Remember that on these calls, you cannot try to sell someone. That may be a surprise to you, especially if you are in the early stages and hungry for customers. The purpose of these calls is to figure out what you can do to attract more people. The insights you get from this person may help you attract tens or hundreds of other customers through better marketing or product improvements. As hard as it is, be patient.

If it turns out you've built something great, there's always a chance they'll want to buy it on their own. So don't force it. (Even though you understandably want to.)

[21]
LINKEDIN

Several early readers of this book who sell to other businesses high-lighted that LinkedIn is their favorite place to find people to interview.

I hesitated because I don't do LinkedIn outreach myself, and I rarely reply to cold outreach myself. But then I thought back to the one unsolicited message I've replied to in recent memory: a student who was interested in getting into investing and wanted to hear about my own experiences.

What made that one different? She wasn't trying to sell to me, and was just looking for advice. It made me feel helpful rather than put-upon.

A successful ask on LinkedIn will call on people's desires to be helpful and feel like they have valuable advice for others. You will want to remember that it is vital to resist the urge to sell on research calls, as that may turn people off from ever accepting such requests in the future. For the benefit of other people building products, respect that people have their guard up on LinkedIn.

Your message should be carefully crafted. The more human, the better, and the more personalized, the better. Do research on the person and their company in advance: Have they expressed frustrations with a competitor? Recently bought a competitor's product? Blogged about this particular problem?

A message that isn't personalized (and truly personalized) is like pouring cold water into a warm glass fresh out of the dishwasher. It will fall to pieces.

Since it isn't a tactic I use myself, I spoke to several founders and consultants who use LinkedIn themselves.

Chris Forster, a media payments startup founder, uses LinkedIn to find marketing leaders at media companies. He then does a screen share to get their feedback on his prototype. This has the dual result of building awareness for his product *and* getting valuable feedback.

Here's his most successful message, sent with a connection request:

Hi [Name], I hope you're doing well. I'm doing research as a tech startup founder on how innovative publishers are reaching new audiences and generating new leads. I'd love to talk with you about this if you have 10 mins for a quick call? I'd very much appreciate it. Thank you! Chris

Forster's messages and success matches with other founders I've talked to who use LinkedIn connections for research recruitment. For your own messages, the points to hit would be:

- Who you are
- Why you want to talk to them (ideally phrased in a complimentary way—note Forster's use of "innovative publishers")
- What you're hoping for from them

Forster notes that he has more success with sending a connection request without a message and then sending a message when the request is accepted. Note that the messages follow a different formula from above: since they've accepted a connection request, they've presumably seen your profile and perhaps clicked through to your company.

Forster's best-performing copy includes:

First message

[Person], good to connect.

It's a huge ask, I know, but I'd love your expert insight and advice on a new tool our tech startup has built to generate revenue from casual readers and with it granular monetization data from audiences. Also creates a stronger pathway to subscription conversion. Hasn't been done before. Pipeline of interest from [brands, competitors, etc.], and others....

Would you have 15 mins to spare on this? Perhaps next week, Tuesday or Wednesday at 2pm?

Follow-up

Hi [Person] - just wanted to loop back. Since I messaged, we've had some productive conversations with the likes of [brands, competitors, etc.], and I wondered if you might have time to share your thoughts and impressions on our [product description] as well? Would you have 15 min next week for a quick call, perhaps Wednesday or Friday at 10am ET?

For more on LinkedIn outreach, Forster recommends guides from the growth consultancy Demand Curve.[1]

FACEBOOK GROUPS AND EMAIL LISTS

Facebook groups and email lists are another great place to recruit, though they can be much more private and harder to find.

For example, a few years ago, my *Software Social* cohost Colleen Schnettler was exploring an idea that would help stay-at-home mothers earn money on the side. For research, she recruited from military base Facebook Groups.

Arvid Kahl co-founded a business built around customer Facebook groups, FeedbackPanda, and discusses various methods in his book *The Embedded Entrepreneur*. It includes guidance for finding and integrating yourself into relevant Facebook groups.

As with Twitter and Reddit, you want to be friendly and not salesy. The formula is:

- Who you want to talk to and what about
- Introduction to what you're hoping to learn about
- What people would need to do

- What the incentive is, if you're providing one. (If you aren't asking people about a specific and current pain, an incentive is more likely to be necessary.)

For example:

Have you bought a car recently? I'd like to build something that makes this easier, and I'm hoping to understand how people make decisions about buying a new car. I'm looking to talk to people who've bought a car (new or used) in the past month. If that's you and you'd be up for a half hour call about this, please message me. I'm looking to talk to 10 people and will give all participants a $15 Amazon gift card.

Notice in the above example how it's specifically asking for people who have bought a used car *within the last month*—not people who've ever bought one or are thinking about buying one, but people with concrete, recent experience with the process.

If you're recruiting for something that someone might use every week, your post should ask for people who have gone through that process within the last week (not people who have gone through it in general).

[23]
EMAIL

This section is intended for companies with an existing product.

I don't recommend doing cold email outreach. Most professionals are used to getting a lot of cold sales emails, and you don't want your research emails getting lost in that.

Email outreach will vary based on who you are trying to reach and when.

Writing a good recruitment email will take refinement and A/B testing on your end. I'll provide a few examples below, with the caveat that you're going to have to experiment with them further.

The highest I've ever gotten my response rates is ten percent, so it's okay if you don't have a high response rate. This is a volume game. If you can get five percent, that's really good.

I suggest filtering your customer list to specific types of people you want to talk to. That could be:

- Time-based: People who've signed up within the last thirty days, people who've been a customer for more than a year, and so forth
- Revenue-based: Customers on a particular plan, customers over a certain lifetime value, customers on your free trial who didn't convert, customers who did the free trial and converted, who upgraded after doing a particular action, and so forth
- Behavior-based: Customers who've used a specific feature, who haven't used a specific feature, and so forth

When recruiting existing customers via email, you want to play up that you're the founder (or developer, or customer experience manager, or product manager, or a title you've made up just for this purpose) and are open to hearing feature suggestions. Titles add an air of credibility and importance to the request.

Getting to request features is usually a big enough incentive in its own right.

The shorter the email, the better. Make sure to use line breaks for easy scannability.

The formula:

- Who you are
- A specific amount of time you want to talk to them
- Why you want to talk to them
- When you want to talk to them
- What you will give them [if applicable]

TEMPLATES

Hi,

I'm the founder of [company] and I notice you [recently started using our product/have been using our product for a while/have used our feature].

I'm hoping you might have 20-30 minutes to tell me more about how our product helps you.

Your feedback will directly influence our roadmap.

You can pick a time here: [calendar link]

Thanks,

You

[Title], Company

Someone you've talked to before in a sales or support setting

Hi [person],

I know we've chatted before [when you signed up for Our Service/over email/through support], but was wondering if you had a few minutes for us to zoom out and give me the broader picture of how [what our service does] fits into what you're trying to do overall.

I'm also interested to hear any feature suggestions or tweaks you might have – or if there's anything you want to make sure we don't change in the future.

I know you've been using the product since [time], and checking in with long-term customers like yourself helps me make sure our plans are aligned with what our customers need.

[Calendar info]

Thanks,

You

[Title], Company

To help with some of their doubt upon receiving an automated email, I've found it helpful to include a PS:

PS: And yes, this is an automated email, but the replies come back to me directly and I'll personally reply.

[24]

SURVEYS

In Chapter 18, I mentioned using short, one- or two-question surveys that are integrated into the product experience.

This section is about using those short surveys as a springboard for further discovery.

If you're using the question I suggested, "What did you use before you used [X]?" here are a few templates you can use to get further context and optionally set up calls.

When someone replies to a short survey, you can reply back asking for more detail:

Thank you for telling me that you used to [use something else/do this by hand/etc]. Can you tell me more about [how you found us/what you're trying to do overall/etc]?

Here is the exact template I have saved in Intercom that I send back when people say "nothing":

Hi,

Thank you for telling us that you didn't use anything before you used [product].

I'm curious—would you be able to tell me more about what led you to need [thing product does] in the first place?

I'm particularly interested in hearing what it is you're doing overall and how you found us.

Thanks,

[Name]

[Title], [Company]

And often, I get several paragraphs back that allow us to build a greater understanding of why people are coming to us.

It's often how we find out that someone mentioned our product in a newsletter or on a blog.

I've even gotten testimonials and sales inquiries from them.

For more on the broader practice of conducting surveys, see Erika Hall's *Just Enough Research.*

[PART 6]
HOW TO TALK SO PEOPLE WILL TALK

This is the most important part of this book.

The tactics you'll learn build toward one goal: creating a bubble of suspended judgement where the person feels comfortable being open.

Throughout this part, you'll also find ways to practice these skills before using them in customer conversations.

We'll go into each one of these in depth:

1. Use a gentle tone of voice
2. Validate
3. Leave pauses for them to fill
4. Mirror and summarize their words
5. Don't interrupt
6. Use simple wording
7. Ask for clarification, even when you don't need it
8. Don't explain anything
9. Don't negate them in any way
10. Let them be the expert
11. Use their words and pronunciation
12. Ask about time and money already spent

Lastly, you'll learn how to pull it all together by picturing yourself as a rubber duck. (Trust me.)

It'll take you some time, and some practice, but I think you'll notice a difference even in your personal life by using these phrases and tactics.

I want you to make me a promise: you'll only use what I'm about to teach you for good.

You won't be manipulative, and you won't use what people say against them. Deploying the tactics in this chapter can make someone open up to you much more than they otherwise would. Someone's confidence is a sacred gift, and it should be handled gently, respectfully, and ethically.

That respect should continue after the interview, too. I expect you to carry through the empathy you build for the customer well beyond the interview, and use empathy as part of your decision-making process.

Before we get into the tactics and phrases, it's important to understand just how much these tactics can transform a conversation.

I got my start doing proper customer interviews in the personal finance industry. In America, people are generally very private about their personal finance decisions and situations. It's an extremely delicate topic, and because of this I had to learn interviewing in a rigorous way.

I didn't realize just how much the techniques outlined in this chapter had woven themselves into my everyday conversation habits until I was at the grocery store a few years ago. I was in line with a dozen items and noticed that the cashier hugged the woman in front of me and they interacted with one another in a heartfelt way. I must have just finished an interview because I found myself asking the cashier about it.

Me, with a smile: Oh, I noticed you hugged her. Is that your sister?

Cashier: No, she's just a long-time customer. I've worked here for a long time.

Me: Oh, you have?

Cashier: Yeah, almost twenty years. I'm due to retire soon. Company's changed a lot in that time.

Me: Oh, has it?

Cashier: [Proceeds to tell me about how the store chain was bought out by another chain ten years ago, how they changed the retirement plan, and how she's worried about having enough income from Social Security, her 401 (k), and her old pension in retirement, and how she's making extra 401 (k) contributions]

This was all in the span of less than five minutes, as she rang up the dozen or so items I had in my basket.

It's important to note that this cashier wasn't just a particularly chatty person. This was my local grocery store, and I'd been there a few times per week for several years at this point. I'd been in this woman's line many, many times, and we had never had more than a simple, polite conversation about the weather or how busy the store was that day.

I went home and told a former coworker about it, and joked, "Do I have 'Tell me about your retirement planning' written on my forehead?" I was amazed that a stranger had told me that kind of information in such a short amount of time.

My former coworker pointed out that it was a sign of just how much interview skills had worked themselves into my everyday conversation style, and how I'd become so much more effective at digging to the heart of an issue without too much effort.

For someone whose only negative mark in their first professional performance review was that I was "abrasive" and was diagnosed with ADHD at eleven years old, it came as quite a shock to realize I now had an active listening conversation style without even realizing it.

That experience taught me how we need to be careful with these skills, and to know when to hit the brakes. It's a person's decision what to reveal, but I always keep that story in mind, and remind myself to back off or shift topics when it seems like someone is on the verge of sharing too much. It's possible to make someone too comfortable and safe. It's always okay to say "Thank you for telling me that. I was wondering if we could go back to something you said earlier. I'm curious about... [some other topic]"

It also reminded me of how so many people don't have people in their lives who will just listen to them, especially about things that are processes or tasks they complete daily or goals that are top-of-mind. The cashier at the grocery store clearly spent a lot of time thinking and worrying about the different sources of income she'd have in retirement and whether they would be enough, but maybe didn't have anyone who would listen to her talk about that.

I find that once you build trust with someone and show them that you are willing to listen, they will talk, because no one has ever cared about that part of their daily life before. Maybe they gripe to a coworker about how long something takes, but they've probably never sat down and had someone genuinely ask them what they think about creating server uptime reports or following up on invoices. They've probably never really talked through where they spend a lot of time, the tools they use, and so forth. They've probably never had anyone care enough to try to make it better for them.

Just being a presence who is willing to listen is more powerful than people realize.

HOW CUSTOMER INTERVIEWS DIFFER FROM OTHER KINDS OF INTERVIEWS

If you're already familiar with other kinds of interviewing, it might be interesting for you to read with an eye for how this kind of interviewing differs. Journalistic interviewing, motivational interviewing, and negotiation-based interviewing all bear similarities to user interviewing, yet also have significant differences.

The first professional interview I ever did was the summer I was interning at the Washington bureau of a British newspaper. The BP oil spill had happened a few months earlier, and my boss asked me to interview someone.

Thinking back, that was a very different interview from the customer interviews I started doing years later.

In that BP oil spill interview, I was digging for information and I was looking for specific quotes that could be used in an article. I already knew about the oil spill, so I wasn't looking to learn their perspective on it. Instead, I needed them to say specific things, and say them in a quotable way.

Customer interviews, by contrast, are all about diving into how the other person perceives an experience, and intentionally suspending the desire to validate your own ideas. Later, after the interview has finished, you can analyze the interview to see what opportunities might exist. (We'll talk about that more in Part VIII, "Analyzing Interviews.")

[25]

USE A GENTLE TONE OF VOICE

In Chris Voss's *Never Split the Difference*, he suggests using a "late-night DJ voice" in negotiations. [1]

"You're listening to WBMT, 88.3 FM..."

Therapists will often speak in soft, slow voices as a method of coregulation to calm their patients.

These techniques help put the other person at ease and create an environment where they feel safe.

Those techniques apply when you're talking to customers, too. A customer interview should be conducted in the most harmless voice you can possibly muster.

Imagine you are asking a treasured older family member about a photo of themselves as a young person. There might be:

- A gentle, friendly tone of voice
- A softness to your tone
- Genuine, judgment-free curiosity

Or perhaps picture that a close friend has come to you experiencing a personal crisis in the middle of the night. You would listen to them, calmly, and just try to figure out what was going on. You probably wouldn't start offering ideas or solutions to their problem, and would focus on helping them get back to a clearer state of mind.

Use that same gentleness in your customer interviews.

It's important to note, though, that you cannot be condescending. I purposefully do not say to speak to them like you would a child, because people have very different ways of talking to children.

Think of your customer as someone you respect and you can learn from.

(Because you should, and you can.)

"Why did you do it that way?" said in a medium-volume voice with emphasis on certain words could make it sound accusatory and put them on the defensive, versus, "What led you to do it like that?" in a gentle, unassuming, curious voice will help them open up.

Try this now
The next time a friend or family member comes to you with a problem, intentionally use the gentlest voice you can muster when you talk to them. The next time, use your normal approach. Notice whether the person reacts differently.

[26]
VALIDATE THEM

Books on product development often talk about validation: validating ideas, validating prototypes, validating business models.

This chapter is about an entirely different kind of validation. It's a pivotal part of getting someone to open up to you.

This chapter is about what psychologists and therapists describe as "validating statements."

These are specific phrases you can use to show someone that you're engaged with what they're saying.

It's okay to have trepidation about what you would say in an interview and how you will come up with follow-up questions. Yet most of what you say during an interview aren't questions at all. Instead, you use validating statements that show someone you're open to what they're saying and are listening.

Your goal is for them to talk as much as possible, and you as little. Aim for the interviewee to do 90 percent of the talking in the interview.

In a customer interview, you use validation even when you don't necessarily agree with what they say, or even if what they say sounds absurd to you. It does not mean that you agree with them. It is instead a way of recognizing that what they think and do is valid from their perspective.

You cannot break that bubble of trust, ever. Even when something wacky happens—which it can.

In a memorable interview years ago, the interviewee suddenly said "Sorry, I'm eating a quesadilla right now," about forty-five minutes into the phone call. Mind you, this person had given zero previous indications that they were eating. My research partner, the unflappable research expert Dr. Helen Fake, just rolled with it and said "Oh, you're fine!"

Notice what she said there. She didn't say, "No worries," or, "Not a problem" or, "Don't worry about it"—all of which either hinge on negating a negative word ("worries," "problem") and thus leave the negative word in the person's mind or are invalidating— and instead told him *he was fine*. Not "That's fine," which is abstract, but explicitly putting the interviewee as the subject and saying that *he* is fine, which validated his state as a person.

It was subtle yet next-level conversational jujitsu that will start to come naturally to you the more you practice this.

You also cannot say that you agree with them, or congratulate them, or do anything that implies that you have an opinion, *even if it is a positive opinion.*

This is probably one of the strangest parts of how to make an interview flow, and for many people, it runs counter to their built-in instincts to be positive and encouraging. The person you're interviewing may ask you if you agree, and you need to purposefully find a way to make that question go away. ("I can see where you're coming from on that. Can you tell me…" rather than "Yeah, I agree.") Agreeing or disagreeing will remind them that you're a human being with opinions and judgments, and the trust will start to melt away. You almost want them to forget you're a person.

For example, when I was interviewing people about their finances, they would admit to doing things that a financial planner or portfolio manager would never endorse. Even though we knew that, we couldn't "correct" them. And we also couldn't agree with them, either. We were searching for their internal logic and thought processes, and if we were to introduce outside information or agree or disagree with them, they would have shifted into trying to impress us and holding back information.

VALIDATING STATEMENTS

- That makes sense.
- I can see why you'd do it that way.
- I'm interested to hear more about how you came to doing it that way.
- Would you be able to walk me through the context behind that?
- I can see what you're saying.
- It sounds like that's frustrating/time consuming/challenging.
- It sounds like you think that could be improved.
- Can you help me understand what went through your mind when [X]?
- Can you tell me more about [X]?
- It makes sense that you think that.
- It makes sense that you do it that way.
- It sounds like there are several steps involved. I'm curious, can you walk me through them?
- It sounds like a lot goes into that.

When using validating phrases, I encourage you to use the word "think" instead of "feel." Some people, I've noticed, will find it insulting to say that they *feel* a certain way, but *think* is interpreted as more neutral and factual.

For example:

You feel the process is complicated.

versus

You think the process is complicated.

Or, better:

The process is complicated.

And remember: most people like to think their job is challenging.

Years ago, I heard someone talk about their recent move to LA. Their spouse was in the entertainment industry and this person was not, and they kept finding themselves struggling to make conversation at cocktail parties.

But they eventually learned a trick. Whenever someone said what they did, they replied with "That sounds challenging," even if the person's job sounded easy or boring. People would open up, because it felt like a compliment, and it would lead to an interesting conversation about the things that person did at work.

What that person found was that encouraging someone to keep talking requires turning the conversation back over to them, rather than offering your own ideas.

Try this now

The next time a friend or family member shares a problem with you and does not explicitly ask you for advice, say "That makes sense," or another one of the validating statements above rather than offering a solution.

Sometimes people say, "I just don't know what to do!" which sounds like an invitation to offer a solution but may not be. If that happens, ask them about what they've already tried.

[27]

LEAVE PAUSES FOR THEM TO FILL

Several years ago, I was sitting in the audience at the DC Tech Meetup. I was there to support a friend who was giving a presentation. And something one of the panelists said stuck with me and is something I remind myself about during every customer interview.

Radio producer Melody Kramer was asked what she had learned while working for Terry Gross, host of the long-running NPR interview show *Fresh Air*. She said that Terry Gross's interview strategy is to ask a question, and then to

wait

and wait

and

wait

at least three long beats

until it is uncomfortable.

"The other person will fill the silence, and what they fill it with will often be the most interesting part of the interview," I remember Kramer quoting Gross as saying.

This tactic of saying something and then waiting at least three beats for the other person to fill it is something I use in every single interview, often multiple times.

The length of what feels like a long pause varies from person to person. The research of linguist Dr. Deborah Tannen shows that people from different American regions tend to have different conversation styles.[1] According to her research, people from the Northeastern US may talk over one another to show engagement, while a Californian may wait for a pause to jump in. People from different continents can have different conversation styles, too: people from East Asia may wait for an even longer pause, and could interpret what seems like a suitable pause to the Californian as an interruption.

A three-beat pause may seem long to some, and normal to others. I encourage you to experiment with this and an extra two to three beats on top of whatever is normal for you.

In addition to pauses, I also encourage you to notice whether you provide prompts and additional questions.

What do you do if the other person doesn't respond right away?

Imagine you are trying to figure out what kind of delivery to order for dinner with a friend or spouse.

Do you say, "Where should we order take-out from?" and let it hang?

Perhaps you add possible answers, like: "Where should we order take-out from? ... Should we get pizza, Chinese, sushi..."

One of the ways people make a typical conversation flow is by adding these sorts of little prompting words when someone doesn't reply immediately.

Maybe the prompting isn't offering answers like above, and is just a rephrase without offering an answer, like "Where should we order take-out from? ... [one-to-two second pause]...Do you wannaaaaa..." [lingering pause with gesticulation]

In an interview, you need to avoid prompting as best you can, lest you influence the person's answer.

When you ask a question, you need to let it hang and let the customer fill the silence.

"So can you tell me why you even needed a product like [your product] in the first place?"

And wait.

Don't prompt.

If they don't reply right away, don't say, "Was it for [use case 1], or maybe [use case 2]…?"

Just wait.

I know how hard this is. In fact, there's a point in the example customer interview where I slipped up and prompted:

Michele: Cool. Was there or is there anything else? Did you have any other questions or…?

Drew: No, I think that's everything I have.

Now, sometimes it might truly get awkward. The person you're interviewing may not respond. If they say, "Are you still there?" you can gently bring the conversation back to focus on them, and say something that elevates what they've already said, like:

- Yes, I was just giving you a moment to think.
- Oh, I was just jotting down what you just said. That seemed important. [Repeat phrase you'd like them to expand on]
- Yes, I'm still here. Do you want to come back to that later?
- Oh, it just sounded like you were about to say something.

If anything, too-long pauses and the interviewer's phrases that follow make the customer feel even more important, and reinforce that they are in the dominant role in this conversation. It puts them in the role of the teacher, which marketing psychology Dr. Robert Cialdini has identified as a powerful way of influencing another person's behavior.[2] You want them to teach you about their view of their process, and this sort of almost-deferential treatment through pauses helps elevate them into that teaching position.

To get the answers you need about the customer's process, you need to create a safe, judgment-free environment. You need to hand the stage entirely over to the customer and talk as little as possible.

And leaving silences without prompting is one of the ways you can do that.

Try this now

The next time you're having an everyday conversation—not a tense conversation, not a pointed conversation—notice whether you ask a question and wait.

[28]

MIRROR AND SUMMARIZE THEIR WORDS

I have a friend who used to have a parrot named Steve.

I remember listening, amused, as he told me about the conversations he had with Steve.

This was years before I learned about active listening. And now, it makes more sense to me why parrots are great conversationalists... even though their vocabulary is limited.

What parrots do is repeat words back at people. And repeating words back at someone and rephrasing what they've said has the magical power of encouraging them to elaborate.

It's a tactic that therapists and negotiators use all the time.

Chapter 2 of *Never Split the Difference* by Chris Voss is a deep-dive on mirroring, as you can also learn about it in *Nonviolent Communication* by Marshall B. Rosenberg.

Consider this excerpt from the example interview:

Drew: I wasn't really seriously considering anything that had a paywall on it because I wasn't sure that it would ever pay itself back off. I knew there were other options out there that would either require moving our storage and our database altogether, which didn't really seem appealing, or having two different services, one to manage each, but then the storage still being just as complicated, only somewhere else.

Michele: It sounds like you had a lot of things you were trying to weigh back and forth about whether you should sort of try to plunge forward with this thing that was already being very frustrating, and then all of the negative effects of switching and all the complications that would introduce.

Drew: Yeah, I really didn't want to spend a whole lot of time investing/building up a new infrastructure for a new product for a new service to handle this one thing. I think the most frustrating part was that it worked and now it doesn't.

You'll notice there aren't any question marks in what I said as a follow-up. I rephrased what he said as a statement, which then prompted him to expand on it.

This is a combination of two conversation tactics: mirroring and summarizing.

Mirroring is repeating what someone has said, and summarizing is when you rephrase what they have said (and sometimes label their feelings).

You can hear another example of mirroring in the sample interview. He describes himself running "running into a lot of walls, jumping through a lot of hoops" and that phrasing is mirrored back for elaboration:

Drew: ...And Firebase Storage just did not work as easily as it was supposed to. We found ourselves running into a lot of walls, jumping through a lot of hoops just to make the simplest things work.

Michele: Can you tell me a little bit more about those hoops and walls that you ran into?

Negotiation expert Chris Voss notes that it's important to say, "It" rather than "I" when summarizing. "It sounds like..." is more neutral than, "I'm hearing that..." since in the second one, you are centering yourself as the subject, but the first phrase centers the situation.[1]

For example, if your spouse or roommate comes home seeming frazzled:

Person: Man! What a day! I had like ten calls today.

You, *mirroring*: You had ten calls today.

Person: Yeah, and then my last one didn't even show up and I'd had to cut the previous call short to make it. If I'd known they weren't going to show up, I could have gotten this thing sorted out, and I wouldn't have to work tonight.

You, *summarizing and labeling*: It sounds like you had a lot of calls today, and because someone didn't show up, you're feeling frustrated that you have to finish your work tonight.

Notice that none of those follow-ups are questions. ("Oh, were you talking to new clients?") The clarifications are simple restatements of what the person has said, without added editorialization of the events.

Try this now

When a friend or family member says something to you about their day, try stating back at them what they've said. Then, try summarizing what they've said as a statement. (Sometimes a gentle upward tone implies interest more, depending on the person.)

[29]
DON'T INTERRUPT

One of the tenets of active listening is right in the name: listening.

As former FBI hostage negotiator Chris Voss says in *Never Split the Difference*, "Contrary to popular opinion, listening is not a passive activity. It is the most active thing you can do."[1]

Listening without any interruptions is the foundation of active listening.

Think about how psychotherapists talk to patients: calmly, with long pauses, and no interruptions.

Now, compare that to how a political journalist would interview someone on TV. They're trying to get information—likely from someone who doesn't want to give it and only wants to speak to their talking points. They likely need to interrupt the person a lot in order to get information out of them. Oftentimes, there's a lot of shouting, interrupting, and talking over one another.

Thankfully, interviews in a business context are usually (always) less combative than that.

You might think you're a good listener. And chances are, you're a caring person who does genuinely listen to people. (The fact that you're currently reading a book about empathy shows that you are a genuinely caring person.)

But I'll also bet you interrupt people sometimes.

Before going into interviews, it's helpful to know what your own conversational baseline is and how much of a natural tendency you have to interrupt so you know how to adjust in an interview setting.

I encourage you to spend a week or two consciously trying not to interrupt people.

If you find this challenging or unnatural, it's okay. This is expected if your personal or regional conversation style tends more toward simultaneous conversation, as documented by linguist Dr. Deborah Tannen. For example, some people talk over others to show enthusiasm and agreement with the speaker. All conversation styles are inherently valid. You only need to make this adjustment during interviews.

Try this now
In your most gentle tone of voice, ask a friend or family member,
"What are you really excited about lately?"

The only things you are allowed to say are:

- *Mhmm*
- *Can you say more?*
- *(Mirroring what they've said)*
- *(Nothing)*

Challenge yourself to talk as little as possible and when you do, to only say things that encourage them to keep talking.

Maybe it's difficult for you. Or maybe it comes naturally. This self-awareness will help you in an interview setting.

[30]

USE SIMPLE WORDING

I encourage you to use simple wording. It helps put people at ease and reduces the cognitive load of answering a question.

Don't worry about using perfect grammar or removing verbal fillers. You might be using a late-night FM DJ voice, yet you aren't really on the radio.

For example, "What are your objectives?" is a mentally more complicated question to parse than, "So, can you give me the big picture of what you're trying to do?"

You can even rephrase after you've started. If you find yourself saying, "So what are you..." you can stop yourself and say, "—Could you tell me more about how your organization uses [this]?"

Jargon may have a place to imply your own in-group association with a particular industry and build rapport, yet I would caution you against using it unless you are certain the other person would understand it. For example, use "software" instead of "SaaS" (software as a service) until the other person uses the acronym "SaaS." Otherwise they might think you are talking about "sass," which is a very different concept!

This practice is known as "code switching." I am intentionally not using it in the main text as it is ironically its own form of jargon in sociolinguistics. I am mentioning it here in case you are interested in the broader concept behind this.

Try this now

Think about the questions you might want to ask a user of your product, or a user of a competitor's product if yours doesn't exist yet. How might you simplify the wording to make the questions easier to answer?

[31]

ASK FOR CLARIFICATION, EVEN WHEN YOU DON'T NEED IT

In a customer interview, you will do a lot of things that may not come naturally in an everyday conversation.

You pause for longer than is comfortable.

You purposefully deflect conversation away from yourself and your own opinions.

You use phrases that show understanding rather than sharing your own similar experiences.

This next tactic is going to seem a bit stranger, and it might go against how you were socialized: asking for clarification, *even when you don't need clarification.*

This is a really effective way to get someone to say more about a topic and dive deeper.

This might sound like:

"Can I just make sure I understand what the steps look like? First you have to get approval from your manager, then you talk to someone in procurement. Could you say more about that?"

Or:

"You just said how you first go to your project manager, then you go ask your manager for permission, then you're allowed to use the p-card, and then you get the receipt in your email, then you have to upload the receipt to Expensify. Does that sound right?"

Or:

"I just want to make sure I have this correctly. First you open up a new browser tab, then you open your email in your browser, then you open the calendar in your browser?"

Maybe asking for clarification intentionally, even when you don't need it, feels weird or somewhat uncomfortable. Children are often eager question askers, and many children are made to feel ashamed about asking questions at some point. In school, the kid who asks a lot of questions for clarification is made to feel like an annoyance and like they're holding everyone else back. Many adults feel like they seem smarter when sharing their own knowledge rather than asking clarification questions. Yet that's the precise opposite of what you should do in a customer interview. You should ask questions and hold back your own knowledge, feelings, and opinions. It's the polar opposite of how many people are socialized. So I just want to tell you that if you have unease about this, it makes sense, and I understand if you're doubting the value of this.

Yet I urge you to give this a chance because repeating things back to someone is a powerful way to show that you are actively listening and to get someone to elaborate.

It shows that you are actively trying to understand how something looks from someone else's perspective. That's why with these questions, you again want to use your most harmless voice possible. You want to make it clear you are just asking for more details, rather than challenging them. These clarification questions should be said *almost* deferentially.

Early in my interviewing journey when I was a product manager, I found myself interviewing a lot of older men about their finances. It was clear they didn't regard me as a peer and could sometimes be quite condescending. This was insulting at first... and then I realized that I could use it to my advantage. I started playing into how clueless they assumed I was as a 20-something woman. It worked, and they told me heaps of things they never would have told someone they respected or wanted to impress.

But that approach only got me so far, and only with a particular demographic. As a founder, it's now critically important that people respect me. If I seem clueless, that reflects on the company and their perception of the quality of my company's products. Now, I strike that balance by elevating them into the role of teacher about *their experience*. In Part VII, which contains the interview scripts, you'll notice this is one of the options for a starting question: "Other customers have told me about how they use [X]. I'm interested to learn more about how that plays into what you're doing." This phrasing establishes my own authority about the field in general while inviting them to teach me about their specific perspective.

This is similar to mirroring, and here's where it differs.

If you feel comfortable asking for clarification even when you don't need it, there's an optional level-up here: restate things slightly wrong. I have a former coworker who would intentionally misstate what the person had said so the interviewee would correct them and overexplain. And they would get incredibly detailed information back.

In the example above about submitting a receipt, if you wanted to intentionally misstate that to get more details, you might say:

"Can I just make sure I have that right? First you go to your manager, then you talk to the project manager, then you're allowed to use the p-card, and then you get the receipt in your email, then you have to upload the receipt to the expense management software."

It's only slightly different—the order of manager and project manager is flipped—but getting their clarification on this gives you a window to, in this case, find out just how the approvals happen for purchasing new software. Understanding that internal process could be critical for converting potential customers.

Your goal is to get the customer talking and get as much detail as possible (on the subject at hand). Restating what they've said shows you're listening, shows that you're interested, and helps you dive to deeper levels.

Try this now

When a friend or family member is recounting a story to you, try summarizing what they've said and change a detail slightly. Notice that they will elaborate and add additional details to the story in their correction.

[32]

DON'T EXPLAIN ANYTHING OR GET DEFENSIVE

If you've created something, there's a good chance you feel some emotional attachment to it.

You poured time, heart, money, and considerable consternation into it. A lot of decisions had to be made. You had hopes that people would use it and were excited about what it could mean for you and your company.

So when someone tells you what you've created doesn't work like it should—or they want to know why it does what it does—you might be quite rationally tempted to start explaining your thought process. You might feel threatened, and it might feel like a personal critique.

However...

When you start explaining how you intended your product to work, or what you were thinking when you built it, you've turned the interview (or the support conversation) on yourself.

By sharing negative feedback, someone is telling you that they hoped what you built would work for them (positive intent!) yet there was a disconnect when using it that prevented them from getting that value they were so excited about. It's a *good thing* if people bring feedback to you, because it means they care about what you've made and the problem they're solving. From this perspective, even negative feedback is effectively a compliment. (Because if they didn't care, they'd never take the time to send you feedback.)

Whenever this happens in an interview, try to reminds yourself that you're there to listen to the other person so you can build a mental model of how things work from *their* perspective.

When someone says, "Why does it work like this?" you should reply with a gentle, curious follow-up question that allows you to learn more about their process.

Some of these follow-up questions to figure out the cause of the disconnect and how you might adapt the product include:

- *Can you tell me how you expected it to work?*
- *I'm curious, can you walk me through what you expected to happen?*
- *What were you hoping to use this for?*

It'll take some time to unlearn explaining, especially if you're the founder.

Once you do, you'll see how it's a key to unlocking new insights about how your customers think and what they're trying to do.

Try this now

The next time someone criticizes something you've done or made, try to dive into the context behind what they were expecting, what they were hoping for, and what they're trying to do. It is extremely difficult to suspend our desires to defend ourselves, and this may take many times before it becomes natural. As a starting point, try using, "Can you just walk me through..."

[33]

BUILD ON WHAT THEY SAY

A couple of years ago, I was preparing for a talk at MicroConf, the premier conference for small software companies, on talking to customers.

I had an outline together, yet I couldn't make the presentation flow. I just couldn't find the glue to make it work.

We happened to be having friends over a few weekends beforehand. I mentioned how interviews can be difficult for people at first because they're different from typical social conversation, and even typical customer support conversations.

Whereas you might usually build rapport through shared experiences or offering advice, doing that in an interview derails it.

The point is figuring out what *they* think and why, after all.

And where you might usually feel like you can share your perspectives on something, doing so in an interview reminds the other person that you're also a person who is capable of judgment and opinions. It tends to close the other person off.

In an interview, your goal is to create a bubble of suspended judgment.

You have to go with whatever they say—even if it sounds wrong or wacky to you. You just have to go with it, lest you burst that bubble.

As I was explaining this, my friend Rocky Gray, now an engineer at Twitter, said "That reminds me of improv!"

He continued, "When I was in college, I was in an improv group. And in improv, you have to just roll with whatever the other person does and build on what they do, otherwise the rhythm will be lost. You can't say 'No.' You have to say 'Yes, and.'"

I've never done improv, but I've watched a lot of *Whose Line Is It Anyway?*. One person could put on a cowboy hat and say they're an astronaut, and the other person would have to find a way to work with that.

With that in mind, you can think of interviewing as a form of acting. Empathetic business-driven improv, if you will.

During an interview, you're trying to build an environment of safety, of trust, of comfort. They should feel like they can be open and honest with you without fear of judgment.

You are a sponge who is there to absorb whatever it is they have to say and build off of what they say.

(And afterwards, you can apply the judgment and discernment skills that have probably served you well professionally.)

Try this now

Notice this in your next conversation. How often do you say negating phrases like "Well, but," or "Yes, but," or "Well, actually…" or "No," or "What you're missing is…"? Just notice. Take mental notes when you feel the urge to say something. Slowly, you'll start to notice when you're doing this. The next time, try building on what the other person says and digging deeper into their perspective. "Yes, and…" or, "It sounds like that made you think…" are two phrases you can use to build off of what they say.

[34]

LET THEM BE THE EXPERT

Consider the following scenario:

You go to stay at a friend's house in a town you've never been to. Cell service is spotty, so you ask them how to get to the grocery store. They tell you to take two rights and a left, and you nod and say okay.

Consider another scenario:

Your partner has a friend visiting. You overhear them tell the person to take a right at the convenience store, pass the dry cleaner and the elementary school, and a left at city hall. You follow up and say that the faster route is to take a right at the first stop sign, go straight through three lights, then left at the yield sign.

(Let's leave aside whether it might be rude to make this sort of correction.)

What's the difference?

In the first scenario, you accept what they say without questioning. In the second, you bring your own experiences and perspective into the mix. You correct—maybe gently, depending on tone of voice —inferring that your perspective is the right one, even if that's the route your spouse takes to the grocery store every time.

(It's also worth noting how one partner prefers landmarks, while the other prefers signage. Different things stand out to different people, even on the exact same journey. Neither is wrong, and neither is correct. They simply exist.)

The idea is:

Everyone is the expert of their own experience, *even if it isn't* factually *correct*.

Your goal in an interview is to learn how they see and experience something. It is not to help them be right, or share your own version of what is right.

In order to make intuitive, delightful products that people want to use time and time again and tell their colleagues about, you need to match the user's version of a process. And you can only learn their process by asking them about it and accepting it without judgment.

Now let's think about this in the context of a user interview.

Let's say someone is telling you how they built their website.

Context for the non-developers: Laravel is a backend framework, and Tailwind is a frontend framework. "Backend" relates to servers and databases, and "frontend" deals with the browser and what is displayed to the user. If a website were a restaurant, the backend would be the kitchen, and the frontend would be the dining room.

You: What tools did you use to build your website?

Person: I used Laravel for the frontend and Tailwind for the backend.

If you're a developer, you're probably jumping out of your skin right now at how wrong this is.

Yet correcting them would shatter the sense of safety you've worked so hard to build in the interview.

To follow up, you might say, "What was it like to use Laravel for the frontend and Tailwind for the backend?"

At this point, they might correct themselves, which is a fantastic

way to get them to elaborate, and is reminiscent of asking for clarification even when you don't need it.

Or they might go into their explanation, and you learn why they
have confused them.

Maybe they meant they started with Laravel first. Or maybe they
genuinely mix up frontend and backend web development. If you're a
programming course creator interviewing would-be developers, this
is incredibly helpful information so you can learn that this is an area
you need to focus on more.

When someone says something that is wrong, you need to say to
yourself, "Okay, that was wrong, yet the point is not them being
correct. How can I gently figure out how they came to understand it
like that?"

Maybe it means digging into sources they used, or the speed at
which they've acquired that knowledge, or the length of time since
they'd worked with the information. Maybe they originally understood it correctly, and then had someone forcefully "correct" them
with incorrect information. We all make errors, or believe things that
are wrong or incomplete despite our best intentions, and we have
valid internal reasons for why those things happened. Even if the
output ends up being wrong.

If you discover an error in your own thinking, you might work
through why it happened from an understanding perspective and see
the context behind why it happened. Everything has context. Other
people deserve this grace, too.

Let's take a less extreme example.

You're talking to a new user of your product—let's say it's that
same programming course. The price of your course is $299. But
they say:

"When I saw the price was $399, I was a little nervous, but I
decided it was worth the investment."

Do you correct them?

No.

(Even though it's wrong!)

You need to roll with it and keep going. And then, keep digging into the reservations they had around the course in general: "Can you tell me more about what made you nervous about it?"

What you can do—in situations like this where the facts matter—is email them later. The next day, after you've sent our thank-you note, you can send a clarification:

Thanks again for taking the time to talk to me the other day. I was just reviewing my notes, and I saw at one point you said you'd paid $399 for the course. I just checked, and you paid $299. [It looks like you had a $100 off coupon for taking a previous class.] I've attached the receipt here for your expense-tracking purposes.

Think hard before you send an email like this, and only do it if it really genuinely matters and makes a difference for them. In this scenario, someone might have a training budget from their employer, and that hundred dollars could make a difference to the person.

But if it doesn't make a difference to the person, don't correct them afterward. If it isn't critically important that they bought a course on a Tuesday rather than a Friday, don't correct them.

I can't tell you how many times people have made errors in interviews I've conducted. Everything from factual errors about the age when Americans are required to take distributions from their retirement accounts to misstating the company name.

When this happens, I like to remind myself of the small general store in the center of the town I grew up in. When I was a kid, the owner of the store was named Wayne, and the store was technically called Wayne's. But the previous owner was named Jack, so most people, including me, called it Jack's... even though I wasn't even alive when Jack owned it.

It isn't factually correct, but it's my experience, and it *feels* right to me. It serves an emotional function: it makes me feel more connected to my hometown and its history. No matter what the factual truth is, that experience is valid. And that is what matters in this context.

Everyone is the expert of their own experience.

If your goal is to get someone to open up and share their experience, correcting them will be counter to that goal. It may be a difficult urge to suppress, if they make glaring factual errors or say things that seem suboptimal to you. It is *their* experience, and to correct them on even the smallest thing would break the rapport you've worked so hard to build in the interview.

Try this now

The next time you find yourself tempted to correct someone, ask yourself if it really matters and if they need to be corrected. Look for the context around why they may have gotten something wrong.

If you find this particularly difficult, *What Got You Here Won't Get You There* is a good read. For those of us who were socialized in competitive academic environments, unlearning the urge to correct others can take a lot of conscious effort.

USE THEIR WORDS AND PRONUNCIATION

In the US, the way people from Nevada and Colorado pronounce their states' names is different from the way people from other regions usually do.

People from Nevada pronounce it "Ne-VAD-ah" and people from outside the region sometimes pronounce it "Nev-AHH-da."

Let's do a little hypothetical and say for a moment that you're from Nevada. Imagine you are interviewing people about their experiences going to conferences in Las Vegas, Nevada.

The person you're interviewing says, "When I first landed in Nev-AHH-da..."

Can you correct them and say, "Actually it's pronounced Ne-VAD-ah"?

Can you gently correct them by simply saying it the local way in your next question?

You could correct them, but it would have a steep cost. Correcting reduces them to a lesser role in the conversation and decreases connection, which is counter-productive.

The goal of the interview is to effectively put them in the role of teacher. They are teaching you about how they view things. Even a gentle correction by phrasing your next question with "Ne-VAD-uh" would put them on alert and spoil the connection you're attempting to build. Even though that is correct to you, and the other pronunciation might be gratingly, offensively wrong.

Reminder: Empathy means submerging yourself in what the other person says and understanding that what they think is valid from their own perspective. To regard someone with empathy is to acknowledge that their experience makes sense in their own mind.

It does *not* mean that you agree with them or that what they are saying is universally true.

So, as weird as this may seem, you should intentionally mispronounce a word to match their pronunciation. (This doesn't mean you need to match their drawl or accent, as that could come across as mocking.)

Don't make a big show of it. Simply use their pronunciation and keep going.

If you pronounce it differently—correctly, in your view—they will pick up on that correction, and it will reduce them to a lesser role in the conversation.

It will shatter the bubble of trust and safety you've worked so hard to build.

The point of the interview is not teaching them pronunciation. Correcting their pronunciation or word choice shatters that illusion. It shifts them into trying to impress the interviewer or defend themselves. That is a distraction from the purpose of the interview, and gets in the way of hearing their unvarnished view.

This goes if they get a brand or product name wrong, too. If you're asking someone about how they tell people about new products for their Shopify store and they mention using "MailMonkey" rather than MailChimp, what should you do?

As strange as this may seem, you need to say "MailMonkey," let them correct you (if they do), and keep going.

Try this now
Notice when someone else pronounces something differently than you. Try saying it the way they said it in your follow-up rather than using your own pronunciation.

[36]

ASK ABOUT PAST OR CURRENT BEHAVIOR

When you're listening to customers, potential customers, or clients, you want to find out what their problems are. You want to find their needs. You want to find out where they're struggling. You want to know if they would buy it and how much they would pay.

So you want to know which features to build and what to write on landing pages and how to structure your product so they'll use it. Customers get to do something faster, cheaper, and/or better, and you get to have revenue. Everyone wins!

The problem is...

You can't literally ask them what they want or whether they would pay for something.

I've noticed some commonalities among people who've genuinely given customer interviewing a go but didn't feel like they got much out of it.

One of them was asking questions that ask the customer to predict their future needs or their behavior.

You need to know whether customers will use your product. So you may have asked them, "Would you use this?" or "Would you pay for this?"

(I used to ask those questions, too.)

If you've ever asked anyone those questions, I'll bet you can tell me how you didn't really get anything useful back. Maybe someone said they would use your product, but then they never paid for it later. People want to be polite, and it feels rude to say no.

It's also cognitively difficult to answer a big, vague question like "What do you need?" or predict the future after hearing a question like "Will you use this?" Humans are notoriously bad at predicting the future.

And if you want to know how they're struggling, literally asking "How are you struggling?" can be a bit offensive, especially when people aren't in a situation where they feel comfortable being vulnerable.

Dave Ceddia, a developer who read an early draft of this book, shared a great example of this:

> "I liked the bit about avoiding implying they're 'confused.' I've had a similar reaction to 'struggle' where I'd ask, 'What are you struggling with?' in a welcome email, and I'd get some replies like "Well I'm not STRUGGLING, but I've just been stuck on this thing for three days."

It's quite possible they're struggling if they've spent three days on something, yet the word also kind of offends them.

WHAT TO SAY INSTEAD OF "WHAT ARE YOUR PAIN POINTS?"

The key is to ask about things that are the symptoms of process pain.

Instead of asking for predictions, ask and listen for *facts*, like time and money spent. Ask people what they have *actually done* in the past or present, rather than asking them to predict their future needs or behaviors. Through their explanations, you will learn about where they struggle ad where they're willing to spend money.

Time, manual solutions, multiple tools, and money are all signs of pain points. Finding those factual details allows you to uncover struggles in a way that's mentally and emotionally easier for them to answer.

Here's how you ask about things that imply struggle:

- *How long does it take to do [X]?*
- *What was it like to get started with [X]?*
- *Can you tell me more about the people you need to work with to get [X] done?*
- *Compared to what you expected, how long did it take to [get started/integrate it/etc]?*
- *Can you walk me through the different tools do you use to do [X]?*
- *Thinking about the whole process to do [X] you've told me about, what takes the most time?*

It's important to dig into how they feel about those steps. They may rather be spending their time doing something else. That's helpful to uncover, too.

If they aren't spending money, and it doesn't take them a long time, that's a bad sign. But if you keep digging into the steps, I bet you'll find something.

ALTERNATIVES TO "WHAT ARE YOUR PROBLEMS?"

"What are your problems?" is another question that is difficult to answer and rarely leads to helpful answers. "Problems" can mean different things to different people and different contexts, and you don't really want to hear all their problems—you just want to hear the problems that are relevant to what you're looking to solve.

Like with "struggle," you need to ask indirectly about "problems." What you want to try to do is discover the overall process and find where they are spending a lot of time, money, or frustration (such as manual steps).

Picture your favorite childhood board game for a moment.

Imagine your customer is on a board game board, and they're moving through the steps of a process. The goal is to figure out the steps of their overall journey and help them move through the whole board faster, easier, and/or cheaper.

Years ago, I was interviewing a relatively new customer. They were telling me about how they used our Census household income data appends for addresses to target marketing mailers. I asked them what they used before us, and they told me how they used to use a competitor where they would have to talk to several different sales-people in different departments (each with their own pricing and data formats) to do something that took just two clicks with Geocodio.

They didn't articulate having to jump through all of these hoops as a "problem" or as a "struggle," yet it was evident it was time-consuming and frustrating.

They trudged through because they didn't realize there could be any alternatives to it. And once they found something that eliminated those struggles (time spent talking to sales reps, time spent normalizing data, all of it for a higher cost), they switched quickly.

THE QUESTIONS TO USE TO ASK ABOUT PROBLEMS

Some of the questions you might ask to find problems without saying "problems" are:

- *Can you tell me about the last time you did [X thing your product would be part of solving]?*
- *[For each step:] How long does that take you?*
- *Who do you work with on [that]?*
- *What tools do you use [for that purpose]?*
- *How much do you pay for [those tools]?*
- *What do you think of [those tools]?*

You want to pay particular attention to:

- What kind of tool they're using for something (Note: I'm using "tool" in an anthropological sense here; a manual process or way of thinking or approaching something can be a tool as much as hammer or a piece of software is)
- What problem the tool solves for them, and which related problems they have that it *doesn't* solve
- Whether they pay for it with money or time, and how much
- What they think of that other tool, and how they'd change it if they could

If you already have a product, you might ask:

- *What do you have to do before [and after] you do [thing with our product]?*
- *How long does that take you?*
- *Do you use another tool for that? [How much do you pay for it?]*
- *What do you think of [tool]?*
- *If you had a magic wand and you could change anything about the [whole process/that particular step], what would it be? [follow-up with why they would change that and what it would help them do]*

ALTERNATIVES TO "WHAT DO YOU NEED?"

If you were to ask customers what they "need," you would be asking the customer to design the features and systems for you. That's a huge mental overhead for them, and it might not even lead to very useful answers for you since they don't have the context behind what's feasible or commercially viable for you to create.

In Chapter 9, we talked about how a product needs to be valuable for the customer, usable by the customer, viable for you to support commercially, and feasible for you to build.

For more on "valuable, usable, viable, and feasible," see Marty Cagan's *Inspired*.

But you may have noticed a problem with those lenses: Customers only know the first two, and only you know the last two. I think this is why people can be skeptical of customer ideas.

Since customers can't possibly know what's viable or feasible from your perspective, it makes sense that asking them what you should build doesn't lead to good results. They don't have the full picture!

But if you don't ask them about what they're trying to do, you won't either.

Try this now

Have you ever asked someone "Would you use this?" or "Would you pay for this?" Do you feel like you got helpful, reliable information back? The next time you talk to a customer or potential customer, ask them instead about what they've used (and paid for) in the past.

[37]

BE A RUBBER DUCK

This last one pulls all these skills together.

And it's also a little silly.

(I promise you it will help.)

But first, think for a moment.

If someone shares a problem with you, do you show you care by proposing solutions?

It is common for product creators to naturally jump to trying to fix people's problems and offer solutions. If you find yourself feeling most helpful when you're proposing solutions or sharing your own ideas or knowledge, that's okay. This comes from a good place.

We create because we care.

Unfortunately, the well-intentioned desire to create solutions can impede your ability to fully understand the other person's experience.

It also changes the subject away from the person's experience. And it does not give you more detail into the other person's experience or perspective, nor does it explicitly validate what they have gone through.

(Maybe you have experienced this first hand in your personal life by being told, "I didn't want you to fix me. I just wanted you to listen.")

One reader noted: "My husband and I recently implemented a way to avoid the 'one-upping' problem-solving of each other's work problems. While we don't do it for every conversation, we have normalized asking each other before responding if the other person wants us to listen or problem solve."

Using the skills you've learned in this part will help you dive into a customer or potential customer's perspective and propose or create solutions that solve their problems better because you understand their problems better.

To build a product, you need to know *why* they experience the problem and *what* they've already tried in order to know *how* to help.

(Now for the silly part I mentioned earlier.)

I often think of the story from *The Pragmatic Programmer* about a developer who would keep a rubber duck on their desk to talk to when they ran into a bug. The idea is that the developer would explain the problem to the duck, and by virtue of explaining the problem to the rubber duck, they would figure it out on their own.

I sometimes find it helpful to remind myself to be the rubber duck rather than the fixer—at least in the half hour or hour while I'm listening to a customer.

Try this now

The next time someone shares a problem with you, notice whether you jump to proposing a solution. Try instead to use the active listening skills from this chapter to help them work through it. Trust that they will find a solution on their own. Picture yourself as a rubber duck who is there to help them find the answer on their own without any judgment or guidance. Mirror what they say, validate their experience, and don't interrupt. Let them find a solution rather than proposing one yourself.

[PART 7]
INTERVIEWS

Knowing which questions to ask is the hardest part of an interview. You probably know you shouldn't ask, "Would you buy this?" or, "What are your pain points?," yet going from what you *shouldn't* do to what you *should* do is a big leap.

This part is your springboard to asking useful and impactful questions in common situations:

- **Discovery interviews,** when you're exploring a new idea and are trying to understand a problem better
- **Switch interviews,** to figure out why someone switched to your product and how you can market it better to get more customers
- **Long-time customer interviews,** to figure out what makes people keep paying you
- **Cancellation interviews,** to figure out why they canceled
- **Interactive interviews,** to test a prototype, wireframe, or live product with someone
- **Card sorting interviews,** to help you understand which problems are high-pain and underserved

These scripts have been refined over thousands of interviews. I have used them with everyone from eighteen-year-old college students creating a map for a semester project, to executives entering a new market, to ninety-year-old men who consult actuarial tables to see if they will leave enough money for their spouse if they die first.

The suggested phrasing has been used and tested in the thousands of interviews I've conducted, yet there are many ways to ask a question. So feel free to make them your own as long as you're keeping the original meaning.

(If you have a phrasing that you think is more effective, please email me! The more we can be a community of continual learners who share techniques, the better.)

I encourage you to adapt the scripts to your purpose. Feel free to delete questions, add questions, translate them, or phrase things in a way that fits with local or industry social norms. The scripts are just a starting point, so make them work for you.

You will likely encounter other situations where you want to interview people. To that end, remember the overall framework for interviews:

- What they're trying to do overall
- The steps they take to do that
- What they've already tried
- Where they spend time and money throughout the entire process
- How often they experience the problem
- How long it takes them

To make it easy for you to use and adapt the scripts, you can find the templates at deployempathy.com/scripts.

38

INTERVIEW PREPARATION

CONDUCT INTERVIEWS OVER AUDIO (AND SCREEN SHARE ONLY WHEN NECESSARY)

Most UX literature will suggest you try to meet in person with people. If you're working with a physical product, this is often critical.

If you have easy physical access to customers, you can consider meeting them in person at a neutral location (say, a coffee shop) or their office or home (if that's critical to understanding the problem). For example, Robert Balazsi, a developer and indie hacker living in Romania, arranges interview with people in his target market in person at coffee shops.

Yet doing in-person interviews also introduces complications to the flow of the interview—even a video chat interview. If the other person can see your face, they can try to read your facial expressions and might hold back if it seems like you aren't interested or are about to say something.

I've found that people are much more willing to be open on an audio call than they are on video. It also removes the stress of monitoring your facial expressions and frees you up to take notes.

In some ways, you want the other person to forget you're a person with your own thoughts and judgments. Doing interviews over audio removes the body language variable and can be a shortcut to deep insights.

Even if you're using a video conferencing platform, make it clear it's audio-only. (Even better, only put the call-in phone number in the calendar invite.)

In some cases, it's helpful to have someone screen share with you and walk you through their process and how they use tools (including yours). Or you might want them to test a prototype. For screen-share calls, see Chapter 43 for the Interactive Interview script.

In-person interviews or observation may make sense for your product, though. If you have easy physical access to your customers, it's worth getting a copy of Steve Portigal's *Interviewing Users*, which focuses on in-person interviewing.

MUTE YOUR PHONE AND NOTIFICATIONS

The key to active listening is giving someone your full attention.

Before the interview starts, put your phone on mute and silence your notifications. It may even help to move to another room to force yourself to adopt a different mindset.

SET YOURSELF UP TO BE ABLE TO FOCUS

If getting yourself into the zone to be a "sponge" that deeply focuses on what someone else is saying is challenging for you, it may also help to be attuned to your body and do some advance prep to set it up to be able to focus.

This will mean different things for different people.

It may mean keeping an eye on how much caffeine you have that morning (as caffeine can lead some people to excited overtalking), the food you eat that day, remembering to take medication or vitamins, or whether you exercise that day. I trust you have figured what your body needs, if anything, in order to be able to focus at this point in your life.

Treat the day you do a customer interview like you would an important job interview or meeting.

AIM FOR FIVE PEOPLE; REPEAT IN CYCLES OF FIVE WITH A NARROWER SCOPE IF NECESSARY

For a discrete, well-scoped problem, the minimum number of people to interview is five.

As Jim Kalbach recommends in *The Jobs to Be Done Playbook*, you might need more interviews until you start hearing the same things over and over again. "You'll know when you've done enough interviews when you can start predicting how people will respond," in Kalbach's words.[1]

If you find yourself with five interviews under your belt and you're hearing wildly different things from each person, that's a sign your problem definition scope could be narrowed down. This is especially common in the discovery stage when talking to people who aren't customers.

See Chapter 16 for more on how many people to talk to, and Chapter 17 regarding research loops.

IT'S OKAY IF THE INTERVIEW DOESN'T FOLLOW THE EXACT QUESTION ORDER

Interviews often veer into territory you hadn't expected. Indeed, that can be the sign of a great interview!

I don't think I've ever had an interview follow the exact order I laid out in the script, and that's okay. Don't feel like you need to force the person to follow your order. Let them wander a bit, and gently guide them to your questions or to the concepts you're interested in as necessary.

It's also common for someone to answer one question in the course of another question. If that happens, don't feel like you need to ask that other question. This is where I find printed scripts with four-to-five questions per page with lots of space in between particularly helpful, because you can jot down notes under another question.

Remember that a fair amount of what you'll say in the interview are mirroring and validating statements. If the interviewer spends ten percent of the interview talking, three quarters of that will be encouragement for them to keep talking about something that's relevant.

STICK TO THE AMOUNT OF TIME YOU'VE TOLD THEM IT WILL TAKE

Most literature will recommend scheduling interviews for an hour. I've found I can get great information in thirty minutes, or even fifteen minutes. Sometimes we don't hit every point in detail, yet I still gain insights into someone's process. I've also had interviews that went for an hour and a half because the person was really open to talking.

Whatever the time you promise, stay to that. I suggest starting with half an hour (if only to reduce the nerves and time commitment on your side about being on the phone for an hour). If you're in a good flow and the person is an eager participant, you can ask to extend. If you find you keep needing to extend, consider asking for more time in the future in advance (i.e. make the calendar invites for forty-five minutes instead of thirty).

The "reaching for the door" question (discussed in more depth in Chapter 45) should be asked halfway through the allotted time to give ample space for the great insights that usually follow.

ALWAYS WRITE A THANK-YOU NOTE

Regardless of whether you have an incentive or not (more on that in the next point), I suggest sending a mailed handwritten thank-you note. Old school and incredibly charming.

The thank-you note can be straightforward. Here is a template you can use:

[Name],

Thank you for taking the time to talk to me about why you use [your product/service]. I appreciated hearing more about [process your product/service solves]from your perspective and how we could improve our product.

Thanks,

[Your name]

[Title], [Company]

PROVIDE AN INCENTIVE OR SEND A THANK-YOU GIFT ONLY WHEN APPROPRIATE

For discovery interviews, you may not need to provide an incentive. If you are finding people on Reddit, Twitter and so forth who are already talking about how painful a problem is, it is usually enough of an incentive that someone else is willing to listen and understand their frustrations.

If you need to do colder outreach (like to an email list or a post on a Facebook group for example), you may need to add an incentive. Imagine you are taking the person out to a coffee shop and would buy them a coffee and a nice pastry, and offer that amount in a gift card. In the US, that might be a ten dollar Amazon gift card (or somewhere that is more applicable to your audience.)

For Switch Interviews and Long-Term Customer interviews, I've found that people who are already customers are more likely to feel uncomfortable or reject a gift card, unless they're college students.

In that case, swag tends to be more warmly received and less awkward. The cheapest swag option is stickers, which I tend to find are met with more delight than I would expect. If you do have a bit more budget for swag, I suggest getting something that is gender-neutral and does not need to be sized (i.e. no t-shirts). Think: hats, pens, notepads. Our current swag is socks and they've been a big hit.

Some companies don't let their employees take gifts, so I always ask "Is it okay if..." because the answer could be no. In that case, just sending a thank-you note (with your business card if you have them) is fine.

For churned customers, a cash incentive is pretty much always necessary. Swag can be taken as a backhanded way of trying to win them back as a customer and I don't recommend offering it. You may have to offer churned customers a higher incentive than discovery interviews. In that case, have your incentive be equivalent to a nice restaurant lunch for one person (twenty-five dollars in the US).

Screen-share interviews are the most complicated incentive-wise. They come off more like an exchange of services than an interview does. A current customer may be happy to do one for free for a product they already use. For a new product, I would suggest offering a gift card somewhere in that ten- to twenty-five range (or the equivalent in your local currency). For non-customers, an incentive is definitely necessary, and should be in the same range.

Fifty or one hundred and twenty-five dollars is a lot of money, but it's a lot cheaper than spending several months building something only to launch to silence. Your time is not free, and it has value. And the disappointment and demotivation that comes from launches like that has a mental cost, too.

Spending a little bit up front to avoid spending a lot of time in the wrong direction is money well spent.

ALWAYS ASK FOR PERMISSION BEFORE RECORDING

Most UX researchers will record their interviews and get them transcribed afterward. Zoom makes it easy to make a recording, and Otter.ai is an affordable and fast way to get 90 percent accuracy transcripts.

As of this writing, Otter.ai gives you six hundred minutes transcribed per month for free with a maximum of forty minutes each per call, as long as you record with Otter while the meeting is happening. (Uploading audio requires a paid plan.)

Always get someone's permission before recording. It is legally required in some countries and US states, so always ask first.

Recording interviews is helpful for analyzing interviews and for when you need to share what you've learned. I tend to find there's a relationship between how robust your process is and how many other people you need to share the insights with. When I worked in a larger company and needed to communicate insights, transcripts were an integral part of that. We would print them and clip out specific phrases and use them to create our journey maps, which we'd eventually turn into infographics that we plastered over the doors of the office or shared on Slack.

If you're a solo/duo founder scenario, or getting this business going on the side, that probably doesn't apply to you, yet you could still benefit from having transcripts to reference.

Our sharing/storage process is that I keep notes in Intercom so my cofounder can read them, and usually (excitedly) debrief him afterward with what I've learned. But just because that works for us doesn't mean it will be the right process for you, and I encourage you to find your own.

DEAL WITH THE LEGAL STUFF, IF RELEVANT

This section is not legal advice. Always consult a lawyer for legal matters.

Some customers may ask for a nondisclosure agreement (NDA) before consenting to an interview. In my experience across consumer and business-to-business companies, this happens rarely, but it does happen.

Larger companies often want interview participants to sign a release in advance. Regardless of company size, if you need to interview people younger than eighteen, you will need to get parental permission with a signed release. See Steve Portigal's *Interviewing Users* for example participant releases, and consult a lawyer if this is relevant to your situation.

Always get permission before quoting someone in a testimonial, marketing, or other context. It's okay to anonymously use their phrasing. For anything identifying or presented with quotes, get written or verbally recorded permission.

It is also worth considering adding wording to your Terms of Service or contracts that permit you to gather and use feedback. As an example only, this is the copy we use, which was drafted by our lawyer (talk to a lawyer for your own version):

Feedback. Customer hereby grants [Company] a perpetual, irrevocable, worldwide license to use any Feedback (as defined below) Customer communicates to Company during the Term, without compensation, without any obligation to report on such use, and without any other restriction. Company's rights granted in the previous sentence include, without limitation, the right to exploit Feedback in any and every way, as well as the right to grant sublicenses. Notwithstanding the provisions of [Confidential Information section] below, Feedback will not be considered Customer's Confidential Information. ("Feedback" refers to any suggestion or idea for modifying any of Company's products or services, including without limitation all intellectual property rights in any such suggestion or idea.)

DECIDE ON A WAY TO CAPTURE THE INFORMATION IN ADVANCE

There are different schools of thought on whether and how you should take notes during an interview.

Some people might find it distracting from fully absorbing themselves into what the other person is saying, and recommend that you record interviews and make transcripts/notes afterward. Some people might be able to type/write notes on autopilot and not find multitasking distracting.

I suggest experimenting with a few different capture processes until you iterate into something that works for you.

A process that worked well for me for the first hundred or so interviews I did was to print out my interview script with five or six carriage returns in between each question, with a single-sided print. This would help make sure I didn't forget any questions, since interviews rarely follow the script in order and participants often answer multiple questions in one response. I would often flip the paper over and start free-form diagraming the process and decision matrices that a person went through.

However, you may type faster than you write, or simply not have a printer, and decide it makes sense to pull up a new doc in your note-taking tool of choice, paste your script in there, and type as you listen. I suggest having a blank piece of paper and a pencil next to you just in case you find yourself wanting to diagram something.

These days, I take notes within Intercom so it's tied to the customer's other communications. I also tag that I've interviewed them so my automated recruitment emails don't accidentally get sent to them again.

If note-taking doesn't work for you, Nugget is a free tool you can use to record and annotate interviews as they happen.[2] You can use Nugget to flag, save, and share important parts of the conversation. (Transcription requires a paid account.)

CAPTURE ANY FEATURE REQUESTS

If the customer requests a feature during the interview, it's important to somehow take note of it in a way you'll be able to access in the future. (Even if you're not sure you would add it.)

You can then reach back out to them in the future for more details once you decide to build that, and/or close the loop when you do. That sort of follow-up—even if it's months or years later—is hugely beneficial in making those happy customers even happier.

In a world where so many companies are actively disdainful of their customers, listening to customers is a competitive advantage. Just by listening, you're already showing customers how your company is different. The follow-up concretely shows that you listened.

ASK OTHERS TO JOIN YOU (EITHER DURING THE INTERVIEW OR FOR ANALYSIS)

Most user research literature recommends doing interviews in pairs. People pick up different things, and one partner may notice something that the other one doesn't.

The interview team should never be more than two people, as it can get overwhelming or intimidating for the person being interviewed

I've personally gotten a lot of value out of being paired for interviews and bringing in stakeholders as silent listeners during the interview.

That, however, may not be possible for a solo founder or in a small team, and it's okay if you conduct interviews solo. It's how I've done a lot of my own interviews the past few years.

Teamwork where you can find it will be helpful. If you are a company of one, consider sharing your analysis with a founder friend. (Just be conscious of the interviewee's privacy. Remove their last name, company name, and any identifying details.)

DON'T DO MORE THAN TWO INTERVIEWS IN A DAY

I encourage you to do no more than one or two interviews per day.

Allowing yourself to completely submerge in someone else's experience can be thrilling yet tiring. It takes a lot of mental energy.

About a year into my own interviewing, I led three one-hour interviews in one day, and was exhausted afterwards. I vowed to never do that again.

Out of enthusiasm for feedback, I violated that rule as I was interviewing early readers of this book, and did six in one day. The interviews were wonderful, yet I was absolutely spent, and I remembered why I made that rule for myself. (I ended up doing thirty interviews over the course of three weeks. That was also a bit much. I'd suggest doing no more than five per week.)

It's also okay to only do one interview a week or even one interview a month. Doing *any* number of interviews is better than none.

USE APPROPRIATE FORMALITY

Feel free to adjust and adapt the scripts as you see fit based on your cultural context.

Most of the scripts in this book are intentionally written in a casual, informal tone. If you are translating the scripts into another language, adapting the tone of the scripts may require additional care on your part.

This book is written from a North American perspective. North American tech culture is generally quite casual compared to other industries and regions, and in North America in general, a more casual tone puts people at ease.

However, in other cultures and contexts, a higher level of formality may be expected. You will need to use appropriate formality in your language to make the person feel comfortable.

Questions that begin with phrases like "Could you tell me..." and questions phrased as statements (such as "I am wondering what led you sign up today") are known as *indirect questions,* and in American and British English are regarded as polite. According to cross-cultural communication expert Samuel Heiter, different cultures have different ways of politely asking a question that can greatly affect the way it is perceived.[3] In some cultures, it may be considered more polite to be *more* direct, even if the words you're using are informal.

Yet depending on where you are and who you're talking to, it may make sense to make your grammar more formal as well.

Entrepreneur Chisa Koiwa, for example, used scripts from this book to interview people in Japanese about education software. When she translated them, she needed to increase the formality of the grammar. In her words, there are four levels of formality in Japanese; the first level would be the level one would use with friends, and the fourth would be the level appropriate to use with the Emperor of Japan. When she conducted interviews, she needed to use the third highest level of grammar; follow-up interviews with the same person could be conducted at the "two and a half level of grammatical formality," in her words.

Similarly, software developer Joy Heron interviews people in German, and needs to use the formal German word for "you" (*Sie*) rather than the informal word for "you" (*du*). This distinction hasn't existed in English for hundreds of years, and is not reflected in these scripts.

NEVER SELL THEM ON THE CALL

This is perhaps the most important point of all:

You can never sell someone during a customer interview.

Selling someone in an interview—or merely saying "Oh, our product already does that" to a need the express that they thought was unmet—will shatter the trust you've worked hard to build in the interview. Don't do it.

You can always email them later.

Let's say they surfaced a task that is solved in another tier of your product. You cannot tell them that in the interview. Instead, email them the next day, perhaps combined with your thank-you:

Person,

Thank you so much for taking the time to talk to me yesterday! I learned so much from you about [problem/process/etc].

I wanted to touch on something you said in our conversation. You said you were looking for something to do [X]. I wanted to let you know that our product has that in the [pricing tier].

I would be happy to talk you through the specific features you'd get access to with that plan if you would like.

Thanks,

You

39

HOW CAN I EVALUATE THIS IDEA?

"Oh, wait, if I could just…"

It's as if suddenly, after wandering through the forest looking for something, anything, that could turn into a business, you have an idea. A kernel of something that might get you to where you want to go.

It's a beautiful moment.

And then, after a short period of time, you think to yourself that you need to figure out if other people see this like you do. If this is a problem they experience to enough of a degree that they'd want it solved in a new way.

This is where this customer discovery script comes in.

(It will also come in if you have an existing product and have gotten enough breadcrumbs from customers about an adjacent product you might build.)

The goal of a customer discovery interview is to figure out whether the problem you think exists *does* exist for other people, and then whether your conceptualization of the problem matches your potential customers' conceptualization of the problem. You also want to get a sense for the different steps involved and the internal/external people involved, which can be make-or-break.

I say "potential customers" with caveats: think of them as stand-ins for your actual future customers, which will help reduce the drive to try to sell them. You can always email them in the future asking for feedback, but again, not as a pitch.

RIGHT PROBLEM, WRONG STAKEHOLDERS

Mike Rogers built Typo CI, a tool that warned developers when they made a spelling mistake within their code. Developers loved it but didn't have the power to purchase it. Mike wrote:[1]

When I first started Typo CI, I didn't reach out and talk to my users. I only talked to a small handful of people I knew quite well.

Recently I followed the advice from Michele Hansen and I started talking to my users. I found out I had a lot of faults with Typo CI which would require a lot of work to fix.

The big discovery I've had was "the users who want to use Typo CI, often don't have the right level of permission within their organization to install it." For example, a developer may want to help improve the spelling within their codebase by adding Typo CI, but to do this they need their boss to install it. This extra bit of friction would lead to the idea of installing Typo CI being suggested, but just never actioned.

I've really struggled to convert users to a paid tier...Unfortunately I've decided it's time to shut down Typo CI.

EVALUATING AN IDEA

The key goals of this interview are usually along the lines of:

- Do people experience this problem I think I've noticed?
- How frequently do they experience that problem/process?
- How painful is that problem/process?
- What have they tried to solve that problem/process?
- How are they currently paying to solve that problem/process (money/time)?
- Who else inside/outside their organization is involved with this process?

Note that I use "process" in somewhat of a broad way: it can mean a defined step-by-step process that takes a person an hour, or it can mean a nebulous process that takes decades.

I used to spend a lot of time interviewing people about their process to retire. That was a very different conversation with people who were aged sixty four versus seventy-two versus thirty-one, who were each facing different complexities within different timeframes.

In a business-to-business context, "the process to schedule an internal meeting" will have a much shorter timeframe than "the process to land a new enterprise customer." Note that a process that takes a day can have just as much complexity as one that takes a year. Regardless of the length of the process, there will probably be plenty of depths for you to explore and treasures to discover.

WHERE THIS FITS IN THE PROCESS

This is generally one of the first touch points in an exploratory research process, along with competitor research and more quantitative market research, analysis of data you might have on hand or be able to find, and so forth. All of these kinds of information play a role in your discovery process.

The customer research process can vary a lot based on company size, and especially so in the discovery phase.

I'm writing this with the potential small software company founder and small teams in mind, though you can adapt it for many other purposes. The need to find a genuine problem that is solvable is high, but the level of research rigor is probably lower than it would be in a hundred-person company, if only for the simple reason that you don't need to widely communicate and defend your findings, and risk aversion is generally somewhat higher since there are more salaries on the line if something goes wrong.

I suggest trying to get people to talk to you first for free, and then using an incentive if you're having trouble. (Having trouble finding people can be a sign that the problem isn't painful enough for people —or that they expect to be compensated.)

CUSTOMER/PROBLEM DISCOVERY SCRIPT TEMPLATE

Remember to use lots of validating statements, mirror what they say, and summarize what you hear.

Starting questions

1. *Hi, is this [person]? Thank you for taking the time to talk to me today. I'm so excited to talk to you. Is this still a good time to talk?*
2. *Before we get started, I just wanted to ask if you had any questions for me?*
3. [Optional: if you promised them an incentive] *I also just want to check if it's okay I send you a [twenty-five dollar Amazon gift card] after we get off the phone here? (More on incentives/thank-you gifts below)*
4. [Optional: if you're recording] *Oh, just before we get started, is it okay if I record this interview? It's just so I can listen to what you're saying and don't have to be scribbling notes the whole time. It won't be shared outside our organization.*

Substantive questions

- *I'm interested to learn more about how you [problem you're looking to solve.] Can you walk me through the last time you needed to do [X]?*

Alternative phrasing for the opening question:
What have you found to be successful about [what you do now]?
Other customers have told me about how they use [X]. I'm interested to hear more about how you use [process/tool] at [company]?

- *How has this process changed since you've been at the organization?*
- *I'm wondering, how often do you find yourself doing this?*
- *What manual steps are involved with [this process]?*
- *Would you be able to tell me what kind of tools you use in this?*
- *How long have you been using those tools?*
- *How did you decide to switch to those tools from the other ones?*
- *Are there any tools you tried but didn't really work that well?*
- *Would you mind telling me how much you pay for those tools?*
- *Is there anyone outside of your team who was involved with selecting those tools/determining which tools you used?*
- *How many team members on your end are involved with [process]?*
- *Is there anyone outside of your team who is involved with [this process]?*
- *Is there anyone you have to deal with outside of your company for [this process]?*
- *What is your least favorite part about [this process]?*
- *This is a little bit of a silly question, so bear with me. If you could change any part of this [process] with a magic wand, what would it be?*

The "reaching for the door question"

This should come after you've covered the above and feel like you have a good grasp of the timeline, roughly halfway through the time you've told them this interview will take. See Chapter 45 for more.

Thank you so much for taking the time to talk to me. I appreciate you telling me how [process] works from your perspective. Is there anything else you think I should know?

When you're actually ready to get off the phone

- *Thanks again for taking the time to talk to me today.*
- *I just have one more question if that's okay. Is there anyone else you think I should talk to about this?*
- *By the way, is there anyone else you think I should talk to?*
- *[If offering an incentive] Is it okay if I go ahead and send you that Amazon gift card now? Can you confirm that [email address] is the right place to send it to?*
- *[If they say they can't accept the gift card:] That's totally understandable. I'd still love to send you a thank you note, where could I mail that to?*
- *[If the interview has gone well:] I've really enjoyed our conversation. If we end up building something that tries to solve it, can I reach back out to you and get your thoughts?*
- *Well great! Thanks again. Have a good one!*

WHAT'S NEXT?

If you're exploring a new product idea, you might find it helpful to conduct research loops where you successively narrow down a problem over several rounds of interviews. See Chapter 17 for more.

[40]
WHY DID THEY BUY?

This script is intended to be used with people who have recently bought something. It could be your own product, or a competitor's product.

This is called a "switch" interview in Jobs to Be Done literature, and the goal is to be able to diagram the process someone goes through from becoming aware they had a problem to solve => deciding to solve that problem => deciding to use a product (i.e., switching from one product to another).

In Jobs to Be Done literature, this is referred to as the Timeline. For more, see Alan Klement's *When Coffee and Kale Compete.*

Accordingly, this is a helpful script to use when you are trying to find more customers. It can also be helpful during the discovery phase to interview someone who has recently bought a competitor's product.

The goals of this interview:

- What was the journey they went through?
- How did they discover your product?
- What prompted them to switch from one provider/tool/process to yours?
- So far, are they satisfied with that decision?

I've intentionally written this as casual and conversational as possible. It is close to what I might actually say in an interview. The grammar is not perfect, and that's on purpose.

Remember that these questions are only a small percentage of what you'd say in an interview. You'll use the skills you learned in "How to Talk So People Will Talk" to encourage someone to continue talking.

The questions in the middle are intentionally formatted as bullets, because interviews rarely follow the questions in order and that's okay.

SWITCH SCRIPT TEMPLATE

This script is indebted to "A Script for Kickstarting Your Jobs to Be Done Interviews," by Alan Klement. [1]

Starting questions

1. *Hi, is this [person]? Thank you for taking the time to talk to me today. I'm so excited to talk to you. I'm [one-sentence introduction]*
2. *Before we get started, I just wanted to ask if you had any questions for me?*
3. [Optional: if you promised them an incentive] *I also just want to check if it's okay I send you a [twenty five dollar Amazon gift card] after we get off the phone here?*

4. [Optional: if you're recording] *Oh, just before we get started, is it okay if I record this interview? It's just so I can listen to what you're saying and don't have to be scribbling notes the whole time. It won't be shared outside our organization.*

Substantive questions

- Ok, so to get started, can you tell me a little about how you got to needing something for [process your product/service helps people do] in the first place?

Alternative phrasing for the opening question:
What have you found to be successful about [what you do now]?
Other customers have told me about how they use [X]. I'm interested to hear more about how you use [process/tool] at [company]?

- *Can you walk me through a little bit what the end result you're trying to get to is?*
- *What other tools or things have you done manually to try to do this?*
- *Can you tell me about when you started thinking that maybe you could or should use something else to get this done?*
- *[follow up: when was that?]*
- *So when did you start looking for something new to [solve problem]?*
- *Before you started using [product], what were you hoping it would solve?*
- *[follow up: Is it helping with what you hoped it would help with?]*
- *Before you started using [product], was there anything you were unsure about or was unclear?*
- *Before you decided to use [product], was there anyone else you asked about it or places you looked for information about it?*

- *Before you decided to use [product], were there any other alternatives you looked into?*
- *Before you decided to use [product], was there anyone else who needed to weigh in on whether it was the right fit before you could use it?*
- *If you weren't able to use [product], what would you do instead?*

The "reaching for the door question"

This should come after you've covered the above and feel like you have a good grasp of the timeline, roughly halfway through the time you've told them this interview will take. See Chapter 45 for more.

Thank you so much for taking the time to talk to me. I appreciate you telling me about how [process] works from your perspective. Is there anything else you think I should know?

When you're actually ready to get off the phone

1. *Thanks again for taking the time to talk to me today.*
2. *Is there anyone else you think I should talk to about this?*
3. [if you promised them an incentive] *Is it okay if I go ahead and send you that Amazon gift card now? Can you confirm that [email address] is the right place to send it to?*
4. [if you didn't promise an incentive] *As a little thanks, I'd love to send you some swag. Would that be okay? We have some [stickers/socks/pens/etc]. If so, where should I send them?*
5. [If they say they can't accept swag:] *That's totally fine. I'd still love to send you a thank you note, where could I mail that to?*
6. *Well great! Thanks again. Have a good one!*

[41]

WHY DO THEY STICK AROUND?

The goal of this interview is to find the customers who are happy and figure out *why* they are happy so you can find more people with similar use cases that are well served by your product.

Outcomes you can expect from these interviews include finding new landing pages or marketing messages that better speak to their use cases, new places to market a product, and ways to make small changes to our offerings to make our service more compelling. The best-case outcomes are that the customer offers to do a testimonial or decides to stay a customer for a long time because of the rapport built in the interview.

LONG-TIME CUSTOMER INTERVIEW SCRIPT TEMPLATE

This will look familiar to the other scripts, with the key difference that you purposefully ask for feature requests in this interview.

When you encounter feature requests, the key is to dive into why they would need that feature in the first place. After you get that context, you can give them details on your company's side: for example, if it's already on your roadmap or already scheduled for release.

If it's beyond the scope for your company, find a nice way to close the topic without shutting them down.

For example:

Customer: ... so that's why we need [something that does X that is wildly outside of the scope for your company]. Is that on y'all's roadmap?

You: You're the first person to surface that, so we haven't really looked at it. Can you let me know how that plays into how you need to [do thing that is related]?

Starting questions

1. *Hi [person]. Thank you for taking the time to talk to me today.*
2. *The goal of this is to kinda dig deeper into what you all are doing overall, and make sure what we're doing is aligned with that.*
3. *Before we get started, is it okay if I record this interview? It's just so I can listen to what you're saying and don't have to be scribbling notes the whole time. It won't be shared outside our organization.*

Substantive questions

- *Let's start with the big picture from your perspective. Other customers have told me about how they use [X]. Can you tell me about how you use [process/tool] at [company]?"*
- *What did you use before [our service]?*
- *What led you to start looking for something new?*
- *Thinking about all of the steps that go into [what they do], what happens before our service/what happens after?*
- *How has the [thing they do that they use your service for] changed since you started using us?*
- *If you couldn't use [our product], what would you do instead?*

Feature requests

Thanks so much for humoring me there on those big-picture questions. I wanted to leave a lot of space here for you to tell me what you think of the product and whether you have any ideas or suggestions or whatnot for us. [Pause]

When they suggest a feature

- *Can you walk me through a scenario where you would use that?*
- *When was the last time you needed to do [X]?*
- *What do you currently use for that?*
- *What do you currently pay for that?*
- *How long does that take you?*
- *How often do you have to do that?*
- *A bit of a silly question here. If you had a magic wand and could change anything about [product], what would it be?* [Pause]

The "reaching for the door question"

This should come after you've covered the above and feel like you have a good grasp of the timeline, roughly halfway through the time you've told them this interview will take. See Chapter 45 for more.

Thank you so much for taking the time to talk to me. I've really enjoyed talking to you today and learning more about how we fit in to what you do. [pause] Is there anything else you think I should know?

When you're actually ready to get off the phone

- *Is there anyone else you think I should talk to?*
- *It was great talking to you today. If you think of anything else, feel free to shoot me an email. Of course, you can always reach me for any suggestions or ideas you or your team might have.*
- [If you have swag to mail out with a thank you note:] *I'd love to send you a little thanks, where could I mail that to?*

WHY DID THEY CANCEL?

Someone downgrades a plan.

Deletes their account.

Doesn't convert on a free trial.

Didn't click the "try it now" button.

Before we dive into the finer points of conducting an interview with someone who has canceled, I want to talk about what lies beneath them: feelings of disappointment for the customer, and in the case of founder-operators, the feeling of rejection.

Cancellation interviews are the most challenging interviews. Do not start with them if you're new to interviewing.

It's possible to interview people who've canceled, but it requires a delicate touch. There are two common reasons why they can be hard:

- The customer hoped your product would solve their problem and it didn't. Or maybe it created problems where there weren't before. Or functionality failed. All of those have disappointment running beneath them.

- You hoped the customer would stay a customer and continue paying you for many years. They didn't. That has rejection running beneath it.

In order to receive the customer's disappointment without getting defensive, it may be necessary to first make space for your own feelings of rejection. Then we can absorb their disappointment without getting defensive and breaking the fragile balance in this already low-trust situation.

THE PAIN OF CANCELLATIONS

For someone who has personally worked on a product (whether individually or as part of a team), someone downgrading/canceling/not upgrading hits deeper and hits differently. This is especially the case for founders. And I think this is something people don't really expect, and in my experience, don't really talk about.

You may tell yourself, "This is just business and I'm being silly for taking this personally," and try to steel yourself and move on. You might think this is overthinking this, over-analyzing it, over-emotionalizing it. I accept that.

Yet a downgrade from your highest-priced plan might feel like a punch in the gut. It might make you momentarily rethink a decision you made to hire a part-time contractor or think about how it puts so many more months in between going from side project to full time. It might make you feel worried about whether this will really work and whether you can really do this. Even if you've been doing this for a long time, you might start to worry if there's a pattern, or if there's something you're missing that threatens the company. Especially if you get two in a day.

Or you might wonder why people aren't converting on your free trial or signing up on a landing page. *Why isn't it good enough? What am*

I missing? When you've poured your blood, sweat, and time into something, it hurts. It feels like rejection.

I encourage you to notice that these feelings of rejection come up. It is *okay* to feel a pit in your stomach or that rush of heat to your throat when you get a cancellation. It is okay.

I put you through this uncomfortably full-of-feelings intro because in order to have a successful interview with a churned customer, you need to let go of the idea that it is a chance to save them and make them a customer again. The goal of a churned customer interview is not to make them a customer again.

(You read that right.)

A customer who cancels can be a sign that something was wrong in the marketing that attracted someone with a use case that wasn't a fit for the product. Instead of trying to win them back, the goal of this interview is to figure out what their use case was and how they came to the product so you can stop attracting people with use cases that aren't a good fit.

You need to attract more of the would-be happy people (which is why I recommend interviewing happy customers as well as canceled customers), and attract fewer of the would-be unhappy customers.

Let's imagine a pizza shop.

The pizza shop advertises in gyms and high school parent email newsletters. They talk to their customers, and learn that the people who are the least likely to be satisfied customers and order again are people who want salads. They are willing to pay up to fifteen dollars for a salad, but they want a lot of options—many more than the pizza shop offers. They find that their highest-paying, most-likely-to-return customers are people who order pizza once a month for their kid's soccer team.

What should the pizza shop do with this information? Should they diversify their salad menu and add more options, or should they double down on the soccer team parents and try to find more of them?

That's a question of strategy and direction, and your answer might be different than mine.

I know what I would do: given no changes in capital, I would stop advertising in the gyms, amp up the newsletter sponsorships, and add menu items that are pre-selected bundles that make it easy to order for a large group of kids. I'd stop trying to convert the roughage enthusiasts, and double down on finding more of the people who match the use cases of the already-happy customers.

There are cases when a product has a demonstrated churn problem, in which case these interviews can help uncover flaws in the product. Before you prioritize every piece of negative feedback you receive, also talk to the people who do stick around. I encourage you to balance cancelation interviews with happy customer interviews to give you a broader perspective on the product. (And it'll benefit your mental health, too.)

No matter what, remember: the goal is not to save this particular person. Consider them a springboard to stopping other people from canceling by not attracting those people in the first place.

The big goal is to figure out how you can attract fewer people with use cases like this, so you can spend more time serving people with use cases that are a better fit for your product.

SPECIAL NOTES FOR CANCELLATION INTERVIEWS

Incentives are key with canceled customers. In this scenario, I would go with the gift card and intentionally not offer swag, as it may be taken as a way to subtly sell them the product in the future.

When you ask people to do this call, aim for twenty to twenty-five minutes. (Schedule it for half an hour, and purposefully give them time back.) Remember: your product didn't work for them and they just want to get on with their work, so don't ask too much of them. Don't worry if you don't hit all of the questions. Ask the "reaching for the door" question around the ten to fifteen minute mark. (More about the reaching for the door question in Chapter 45.)

CANCELED CUSTOMER INTERVIEW SCRIPT TEMPLATE

You'll notice this script has a lot of similarities with the other interview scripts. This one is sort of like a discovery interview but in reverse: rather than trying to figure out the inertia that led them to switch to a product, you're trying to find the reverse so you can prevent that from happening with someone else.

Validating statements are more important than ever in this interview. It's critical that you just listen and do not get defensive or interrupt them in any way, or go into any explanations of what you intended when you build something. Their perspective is the focus here, and you need to try to avoid the urge to defend the product. (As hard as it is!)

Starting questions

1. Hi, is this [person]? I really appreciate you taking the time to talk to me today. I understand you recently canceled [product].

2. I appreciate your generosity in helping us understand what went wrong so we can prevent other people from having the disappointing experience you've had. Before we get started, I just want to say explicitly that this isn't a sales call, and nothing you say here will be used for sales purposes. It's just to listen and understand your perspective.

3. [Optional: if you promised them an incentive, which you usually would in this scenario] *I also just want to check if it's okay I send you a [twenty five dollar Amazon gift card] after we get off the phone here?* [More on incentives/thank-you gifts specifically in a churn situation below]

4. [Optional: if you're recording] *Oh, just before we get started, is it okay if I record this interview? It's just so I can listen to what you're saying and don't have to be scribbling notes the whole time. It won't be shared outside our team.*

. . .

Deal with the disappointment first

- *I understand you canceled. Can you just walk me through what led to that? [Be ready to listen a lot here.]*
- *Were there other situations that contributed to you thinking maybe this wasn't the right fit?*
- *Was there anyone else involved in the decision to cancel?*
- *How did the process to cancel go?*

Why they came to you in the first place

- *I'm interested to learn more about how you [problem you're looking to solve.] Can you walk me through what that process looked like before you used [product]?*
- *Can you just tell me a little bit about why your company does [this process] in the first place?*
- *Who was it that made the decision to use [your product]?*

What they'll use/do next

- *Do you know what you will replace [our product] with?*
- *Can I ask how you came across [that product]?*
- *Is there anyone outside of your team who was involved with selecting those tools/determining which tools you used?*
- *Is there any chance you would tell me how much you're paying for [the new tool]?*

The "reaching for the door question"
This should come after you've covered the above and feel like you

have a good grasp of the timeline, roughly halfway through the time you've told them this interview will take. See Chapter 45 for more.

Thank you so much for taking the time to talk to me. I've learned so much from you today. Is there anything else you think I should know?

When you're actually ready to get off the phone

- *Thanks again for taking the time to talk to me today. I appreciate you generously taking the time to walk me through why [product] didn't work for you. I've learned a lot about how we can improve.*
- *Is it okay if I go ahead and send you that Amazon gift card now? Can you confirm that [email address] is the right place to send it to?*
- [If they say they can't accept the gift card:] *I totally understand. I'd still love to send you a thank you note. Where could I mail that to?*
- *I appreciate your time today. Thanks again.*

[43]
WHAT DO THEY THINK?

Sometimes it's helpful to put something in front of someone and get their thoughts. Whether that's a website or a piece of paper with a sketch, different insights can come out when someone has something with which to interact.

Similar to usability testing, doing an interactive interview involves putting a "physical" product in front of someone for them to explore in a guided way. This can be a landing page, a prototype, a wireframe, or anything else they can see and interact with.

What I discuss here is more akin to what UX literature would describe as prototype testing, except applied to new and existing experiences alike. This section is more focused on business validation and solution evaluation cases, with a sprinkle of usability.

Usability testing is generally focused on user interface factors and whether the mental model of the product matches the user's mental model of a specific problem, but less so on discovering overarching goals (jobs) and processes. For example, usability testing encompasses whether people can locate a button (a signifier), whether a dashboard permits someone to delete their account (affordances), the kind of content a user might expect to find in the navigation, and many other scenarios.

Accessibility design and testing are related. That includes but is in no way limited to, for example, testing with screen readers or on slow internet connections. Accessibility-related and usability-related issues will often come up in this type of session, even though it is not the primary purpose. For more on accessible design, please see the Further Reading chapter at the end of this book and the A11y Project (a11yproject.org).

You can find deeper insights about people's processes and organizational dynamics that will help you identify unanticipated snags that might reduce conversions or successful use of the product.

It can be used for landing pages to see why people aren't buying, to understand difficulties people might have with using a tool, to see why people keep emailing support about something that they can do on your website without you, to test a prototype, to see them implement your service, and more.

Remember Marty Cagan's four elements of a successful product—usable, viable, feasible, and valuable?

Interactive interviews are often used for *usability* testing, yet they can also be used for testing value.

Hua Shu has been running a pilot of her brand design tool for small businesses. For one hundred dollars, customers go through a guided process through her software to create a logo and branding. They get to see what customers like, where they struggle, *and* they get paid for it. She's testing usability and value at the same time.

Interactive interviews can even reveal fundamental flaws in your thinking.

I'll give you an example.

In late 2017, I decided to act on a long-standing, frequent customer request. For years, we'd had potential customers ask us if they could process patient addresses.

The data handling rules for health-related data in the US are strict, and this meant rebuilding our infrastructure from scratch to make it comply. Given the expense and time required on our end, we put a lot of research into it. We did surveys, interviews, competitor research, and market sizing. We hired external consultants to ensure compliance.

But we figured that since people wanted the same process as our existing product, we didn't do much on the usability testing side. We'd just mirror the UI, with different piping under the hood.

I continued regular conversations with potential customers and surveys through the development process, getting more clarity on things like pricing—down to which plans they intended to buy and trying to effectively presell the product.

Almost a year later, we launched. And emailed the hundreds of the people who'd said they'd definitely use it.

And waited.

And... nothing.

Not even on our lower-cost pay-as-you-go plan.

I got responses from a few people, and they said it was still working its way through internally.

Hmm.

A week went by.

Given the enthusiasm we'd received to that point, I was confused, and knew we'd missed something. So I went to Reddit, found the HealthIT subreddit, and told people I'd give them a twenty-five dollar Amazon gift card for helping us test our site. I found developers, data analysts, and even hospital executives. (See Chapter 19.)

The first test went well—which was a disappointment, since we needed to learn. Nothing was confusing on the site, it was clear what it was and why it was a better product than other options, and the person was excited about it.

And then at the end I asked, "Let's say you decided to use this product. What would you do next?" expecting them to click on the "sign up" button.

"Oh, I'd go talk to our legal department."

It was expected that legal departments would be involved. We'd even designed a whole new onboarding flow specifically for uploading the required documents before using the product. We had a new section on the website devoted to security and different measures we'd taken to ensure compliance.

But something in their tone of voice told me this wasn't their favorite step in the process. So I decided to seek clarification even though I thought I knew the answer.

Me: "Oh?"[Pause]

Person: "Yeah, I'd have to go talk to legal. And they'd probably have to do a security review, in addition to contract review. Man, sometimes that takes six months, or longer."

Oh, %&$*.

We knew legal would be involved. We knew security reviews would be involved. We did not realize it would be a six-month-plus process... even for a product that would cost them $500 a year.

Our pay-as-you-go tier only works because it's self-service. Doing that level of legwork for a lower-tier plan just wasn't feasible for us.

Surviving six months of reviews and negotiations for a plan that required us to keep very expensive servers running even when we didn't have any customers? That wouldn't work, either.

The next screen share test revealed the same thing. And the one after. And the one after.

And the one after.

We gave it another week.

We'd nailed most of viable, valuable, usable, and feasible: it was valuable for the customer, usable, and feasible for us to build.

But was it viable for us as a business when the rubber hit the pavement? Turns out, no. A sales cycle of six months would kill us.

A month in, we decided to scrap the pay-as-you-go tier, and only offer the product as an enterprise option. (The benefit of this was that because of the way this plan is built, we only incur costs when we have a customer.) For months, this basically meant the product was a landing page only with no customers, effectively dormant.

Then one person signed up... and another a few months later.

It took about a year for the product to find its footing. It's now our fastest-growing product and contributed significantly to our 56 percent growth rate last year.

The vast majority of those customers did indeed require months of discussions and reviews. One review lasted a year and a half. (Though another six hours—but that's an anomaly.)

The moral of the story?

Get your product in front of people. Get your prototypes, your drawings, your products that have been around for five years, get them all in front of people.

And don't just ask about the product. Don't ask them if they would use it or if they would buy it. Instead ask about the decision process, the other stakeholders involved, and what other complications might come up—the parts that have nothing to do with technology.

SPECIAL NOTES FOR INTERACTIVE INTERVIEWS

If you are doing this interview as a screen share, I suggest setting the call as audio-only and granting the person screen share permissions, reducing the need for visual interaction. I also strongly suggest recording these sessions to give your brain the most amount of space to absorb what the person is doing, where they hesitate, and so forth. (Remember to always ask for permission before recording.)

I would suggest scheduling these sessions for half an hour. An hour is the absolute most, as it might be tiring for both you and the participant. (I have observed that screen share tests can be more mentally taxing than interviews.)

If this is a project where you've specifically recruited people, offer a monetary incentive. Reviewing a product, even if digital and intangible, feels different to people than a conversation does—it feels more like work. The social dynamic is that they're doing you a favor, so to match that feeling. Ten to twenty five dollars to Amazon is usually enough (or the equivalent in your local currency). I wouldn't offer swag in this scenario.

By contrast, it's different when someone (customer or not) asks you for a feature or raises an issue with how something works. For example, a potential customer asked us if we had an integration with a specific ad platform. I'm unfamiliar with ad platforms, so I asked them to walk me through what they were trying to do so we could consider what the scope of it would even be. Since there was a strong incentive on their end, the dynamic was more that we were doing them a favor than the other way around. It would have been awkward to then offer them a gift card. (Social dynamics are important.)

A key way this differs from other types of interviews is that it's more observational, with the person driving the flow. Most of the session is spent listening to their narration and asking things like, "Is that what you expected to happen?" and "Can you tell me more about why you'd want it to do that/why you thought it would do that?"

If the person asks you what will happen, you'll need to deflect it back to them. For example:

Person: "Will this let me do [X]?

You: "Can you tell me more why you'd want to do that?"

The hardest part about this kind of interview is watching someone struggle through something without giving them hints or prompts, and not giving them answers when they ask how to do things.

It's hard to resist, but you can do it!

You will learn so much from this kind of test if you can manage to tamp down your desire to rescue them from confusion in the moment. Remember, the confusion you're seeing on screen is probably replicated by dozens or hundreds of users you've never been able to observe and who have shown up in your data as drop-offs, so being patient and not jumping into help in the moment will help many more people in the future.

(And if you fix something later, it would be nice of you to email this person to tell them that they helped improve it for others. That kind of follow-up will go a long way.)

AVOID THE WORD 'CONFUSING'

A key goal of this is to figure out what is confusing about what you've built. (I'd say, "What if anything," but in my years of being in this space, I've learned there's always something.)

However...

I strongly advise you not to use the word "confusing," unless the person themselves uses it.

In the same way that some people might be offended by the question "How do you feel about that?" and react better to "What do you think about that?" some people may find it off-putting for someone else to imply they were confused, as if it implies something they did wrong.

Instead, I have gotten better reactions to phrases like "makes sense." For example:

Is there anything on this page that doesn't make sense?

What part of that process didn't really seem to make sense?

I notice you hesitating. Is there something that doesn't make sense?

I have noticed that sometimes "confusion" is something inflicted upon us by an external force, whereas whether something "makes sense" assumes our inner concept of what is sensical is the correct one.

The exception to this is if the person uses the word "confusing" themselves and you use it in a mirroring context. For example:

Person: "Jeez, that form is confusing!"

You: "Can you say more about what was confusing about the form?"

INTERACTIVE INTERVIEW SCRIPT TEMPLATE

As with the other scripts, this script is intended as a springboard to build your own script. You can adapt the questions and wording to fit your purposes and cultural/linguistic context.

1. *Thank you so much for taking the time to do this with me today. Is this still a good time?*
2. *I've planned that this will take about half an hour. [After that, I'll send you the gift card as promised.]*
3. *Before we start, do you have any questions for me?* [pause]
4. *Do you mind if I record this session?* [quickly] *That'll just make it easier for me to review it later, and it won't be shared externally.* [pause]
5. *So, before we get started, I want to just make sure it's super clear that we're testing the site, not you. You can't do anything wrong. The more honest you can be is helpful for us. If something doesn't make sense to you, there's a good chance it wouldn't make sense to someone else, and we'd rather figure that out now rather than when we launch it and accidentally confuse a whole bunch of people. So your honesty is super helpful.* [pause]
6. *So as you're going through the site, please narrate out loud everything you think as you think it. Remember, you can't offend me.* [pause]

Acclimating

- *Okay, cool, let's get started. I've just given you screen share permissions. Can you try to share your screen? Feel free to close any tabs or anything that you wouldn't want someone else to see.*
- *Okay, looks like I can see your screen. Great.*

First Questions

- [If you want to see how they find your product] *If you wanted to go to [our website], how would you do that?*
- *Can you take a look at this page and tell me what you think you can do here?*
- *What do you think this product does?*
- *Thinking big picture, where might this product fit into your process? What might you need to do beforehand, and what would come after?*

Expectations

You will likely need to repeat this cycle several times—think, key calls-to-action, key features, and so forth.

- *If you clicked on that button, what would you expect to happen?*
- *Go ahead and click it.*
- *Was that what you thought would happen?*

Task Analysis

This may be repeated in several loops to analyze key actions. For example, for Geocodio, this might be "create an API key" or "geocode a spreadsheet."

- *Let's say you wanted to [do thing your product does]. Without doing it, can you tell me where might you go to do that?*
- *Okay, can you show me where you think you would do that?*
- *Before you click, can you tell me what you expect to happen?*
- *Is that what you expected to happen?*
- *Can you go ahead and [do the thing]?*
- [Observe them going through process. If they hesitate, ask them why.]

Decision Process

- *What would you want to know about this product before deciding to use it?*
- *How would you find that information?* [go through the "Expectations" process above]
- *Let's say you decided you want to use this product. What would your next step be?*
- *Would you need to talk to anyone else in your organization before using it?*

Purchase Process

- *Let's say you have approval to buy this product. [I'm going to give you a fake credit card so you can do that.] What would you do first?*
- [Watch them go through the purchasing process]
- [Before they click to buy] *What would you expect to happen once you click "buy"?*
- [After they "purchase"] *Was that what you expected to happen?*
- *If you wanted to then use the product, what would you do?*

Magic Wand

I have a bit of a lighter question, so bear with me here. If you had a magic wand, and you could change anything about this site or product or anything else, what would it be? It can be multiple things.

Wrap-Up

- *Thank you so much for taking the time to do this today. I just have one more question. Is there anything else you think I should know about what you saw today?* [note: this usually elicits fewer reactions than in an interview because of the Magic Wand question, yet it's still worth asking.]
- *Thanks again for doing this. You can stop sharing your screen now, and I'm going to go ahead and send you that gift card now if you can stay with me for a moment.*
- *[email] is your email, right? Okay, it's on its way now. I'll just hang here with you for a moment while we wait for it to be delivered. [pause, let them offer any other thoughts that may have come to them]*
- *Did it arrive? Great. Okay. Thanks again!*

WHAT TO PRIORITIZE?

In the same way that asking customers about their problems can seem like a strange concept at first, I want to tell you that you can also ask customers to prioritize for you.

Now, you're not going to give them full control over the roadmap (even if that's a mental roadmap).

Yet you can ask them to prioritize different problems to give you a better sense of which problems have an acute, unmet need.

Card sorting is a way to ask a customer to prioritize different problems.

It's sometimes used in the context of specific features, especially as an internal decision-making tool by product teams in larger companies.

Here, it can be used as a tool to get a better sense of which problems are currently underserved and which might have the highest willingness to pay.

It can be helpful to visualize them as cards. For example, you could make a Trello board with different cards for each problem, and ask the customer to drag them into a new column, prioritized.

I suggest doing this with customers you've already talked to.

EXAMPLE CARD SORTING ACTIVITY

Let's say you've done five interviews with customers about their experiences with invoicing platforms, and you've got a long list of problems they're trying to solve. Your list looks something like this:

1. A customer asks for an invoice to be adjusted to add their VAT number
2. The PO on a recurring invoice has expired
3. An invoice needs to be prorated
4. Creating a new invoice for a customer
5. Sending a quote to a customer
6. Invoicing a customer who uses a procurement portal

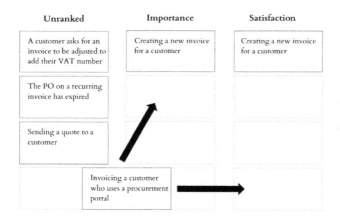

In the example above, all of the cards started in the "Unranked" column. When dragged over, the card is duplicated, and should appear in both Importance and Satisfaction. Here, creating new invoices is both important to the customer and they are satisfied with how they do that. Submitting invoices to customers who use procurement portals is also important (though less so), yet they are much less satisfied. This is an opportunity to dig deeper. "Can you tell me why you put 'Invoicing a customer who uses a procurement portal' in the bottom of the Satisfaction list?"

What can be especially illuminating about this is the customer providing their own input on the problem and elaborating further, giving you greater insight into how they understand the problem and how well it's currently solved. It's helpful for both prioritization and further problem clarification.

As there is a visual element here, I strongly recommend recording this session. You will want to create a new board for each customer.

CARD SORTING INTERVIEW SCRIPT

- *Thank you for taking the time to help me today.*
- *Before we start, is it okay if I record this session?*
- *I'm going to show you a [Trello board] with different needs that you and other customers have told us about. We're hoping to understand better which of these problems are the most important for our customers and aren't solved very well by existing tools.*
- *I'm going to ask you to make two rank-ordered lists: one with how important that thing is to you, and the second with how well you think your current tools support you in doing that.*
- *This is all your own perspective, and you can't do anything wrong.*
- *If you can narrate out loud as much as possible, that's helpful for us to better understand how you approach this.*

Acclimating to the board

- *First, looking at all of these different pieces of [accomplishing the process], does it look like anything is missing?*
- *Would you change or edit any of these items?*
- *Can you read each card and let me know what you interpret them to mean?*

Mostly you will be listening and watching. Listen for when they make corrections to what the cards say and add details about how they perceive those problems.

After they finish sorting the cards, you can ask them questions like...

- *Can you tell me what led you put that card [first/last]?*
- *It seems like [card] is important to you, and you aren't happy with the tools you currently have to do it.*
- *What would the consequences of not being able to do [top ranked card] be?*

And lastly, the "reaching for the door" question

- *Thank you so much for all of this. Is there anything else you think I should know?*

Wrap-Up

- *One last question. Is there anyone else you think I should talk to?*
- *Thank you so much for taking the time to do this today. You can stop sharing your screen now.*
- *Feel free to email me if anything else comes to mind.*
- *Good talking to you. Thanks again!*

[45]

THE "REACHING FOR THE DOOR" QUESTION

When I plan customer interviews, I plan that the first half of the interview will be spent on questions in my script and leave the second half completely open for what comes after what I call the "reaching for the door" question.

For example, if it's an hour-long interview, I'll ask this at the thirty-minute mark.

This question is a famous question among user researchers and comes from the medical world. As Steve Portigal relates in *Interviewing Users*, people will save the most crucial information for the last moment.[1] They'll go through all of the questions with the doctor, compliantly answering questions about sleep, caffeine, medications, and so forth. And it is only when the patient is reaching for the door that they will reveal what is actually going on.

This question is simple, and you ask it in the most harmless voice you can possibly muster:

"Thank you so much for taking the time to talk to me today. I learned a lot from you today. (breath) Is there anything else you think I should know?"

And then you wait.

And the person might say, "Well…" or "No…"

(Nine times out of ten, I've found they say, "No," or "Not really"... but there's a pause...)

And you wait,

again,

for them to fill it.

Don't prompt by saying things like "Anything about process, or tools, or feedback, or..." JUST. WAIT. Do not fill the space. Do not prompt.

It's hard! I know!

You can do it.

Now, if fifteen seconds goes by—and a real fifteen seconds, not a five second pause that feels like thirty seconds—and they say, "Are you still there?" you can say, "Oh, yes, I thought you were about to say something," or something else that throws the conversation ball back to them and elevates the importance of what they've said.

Some of those phrases include:

- *Oh, sorry. I was just taking notes on that last thing you said. [Repeats phrase]*
- *Yes, I was just giving you space to think. It's okay if you need a moment.*

You can also pivot it toward yourself, in case they seem particularly reluctant. Some people may not feel comfortable opening up more until their interviewer has shared some information. (Just be careful with how much you share.) I would be careful not to phrase this with the word "question" as people may interpret that literally, as if they are supposed to have a written question in front of themselves for you.

- *Perhaps there are some things you're wondering about from my side?*
- *Is there anything you're curious about from me?*

They might genuinely not have anything to say, and that's okay. In that case, you can say, "Well I can give you some of your time back. I really appreciate you taking the time..." and go into your closing script.

Some people may have already said what they had to say in the beginning. Or are busy. Or aren't really feeling the whole interview thing. And that's fine.

Nine out of ten times, people take the "reaching for the door" question as a springboard to share what they really think about the topic.

More often than not—people will have something to say – and oftentimes, in a big way.

I have found that interviews that felt like I was drawing blood from a stone will turn on a dime at this point, and out flow some absolutely incredible insights about the person's process, fears, hopes, and ideas.

Sometimes it does require asking a few times in different ways. If you've already asked "Is there anything else you think I should know?" and don't get much back, you can go into your closing script and then rephrase it:

- *Is there anything else you want to add?*
- *Is there anything you hoped we'd talk about?*
- *I just want to check, were there any questions or thoughts you had for me?*
- *Is there anyone else you think I should talk to about this?*

I did an interview recently where someone answered "No" to all of those questions and didn't elaborate the first two times... and then finally opened up the third time I asked.

I've thought a lot about why this is.

Do you want to know my theory?

Interviews can be so powerful because many people aren't used to being listened to. In a business context, you're probably asking them about a frequent process they've never really sat down and diagrammed for anyone. They've probably never had anyone really care enough to ask them for the nitty-gritty details. So when they have someone who is ready and willing to listen to them, the floodgates open.

From there on, you can just do a lot of listening with small follow-up questions like, "Can you say more about that?"

I find that my diagramming of the person's process tends to go into turbo mode at this point. I often add new details to previous questions and really start to draw out the steps a person goes through, how much time/energy/frustration go into them, and so forth. (If you're printing out your scripts, this is why leaving lots of line breaks in between questions and leaving one side of paper blank is helpful: you don't have to go scrambling for another piece of paper.)

It might be scary to think that this part of the interview is unscripted and worry about what you might say. If that sounds like you, you might jot down a couple of validating statements to use at the top of your script as a little phrase bank for yourself if you start to panic.

This might be a good time to tell you a secret about interview scripts.

The first half of the interview—the part where you're following the script—is almost less important for the actual answers you get than for the rapport you build. The interview script serves two purposes: it directs the interview and helps you answer your questions, and it also primes the person to think about this topic and establishes trust that you are willing to listen to them.

This is why I think it's important that you have a script and ask good questions, and it's just as important to focus on how you ask those questions. It's okay to feel like you need to spend a lot of time fussing over your questions. Yet your questions don't have to be perfect. A grammatically clumsy question asked in a caring way beats out a grammatically perfect question asked in a cold way every time. Ask your questions gently and curiously, like you might a grandparent about a picture of themselves as a child.

So by the time you get to the "reaching for the door" question, they've got their mind going about this topic, they trust that you are interested in what they have to say about it, and more often than not, the floodgates will open. And then you just need to listen.

You'll notice that the scripts include "Is there anyone else you think I should talk to about this?" in the end, around the "reaching for the door" question. That question is helpful in its own right, and it can also serve the same purpose.

If you're having trouble getting someone to open up, asking who else you can talk to is both a springboard to your next interview and a way to get them to think out loud about the problem. It can lead to a name *and* elaboration.

[46]

HOW TO ASK PEOPLE HOW MUCH THEY WOULD PAY

One of the things you most want to know when creating a product is whether anyone will pay for it.

The thing is, like asking "What are your problems?", asking someone, "Would you pay for this?" or, "What would you pay for this?" rarely leads to a useful answer.

It yields an *opinion*—perhaps an opinion designed to protect the other person socially as they may not want to hurt you—and what you need are *facts*.

That's the wonderful thing about asking about what people's existing goals are, what they're already using, what they've tried, and so forth: you're asking about facts and someone's existing behavior, rather than asking for someone to predict their future behavior.

The good news is, there are a bunch of ways to figure out willingness to pay. And none of them require the person to predict their future behavior or put them in an awkward social situation where they might be tempted to give you a nice answer to be polite.

There are plenty of ways to do this with live tests, and these tactics are extensively documented elsewhere: price tests, smoke tests, the list goes on. These tools are worth being aware of and using when necessary.

These tools in particular are good with solving the "people are just being nice" problem that *The Mom Test* talks about:

You: Would you pay ten dollars for this?

Person: Sure, yeah.

You: Ok, pay me ten dollars right now.

Person: Oh, uhhh....

Asking about a specific price can often cause awkwardness and lead to not very good data in return.

How you can ask people what they would pay...without asking them what they would pay?

At a high level, the way to ask someone what they'd pay without asking them what they'd pay is to ask what they're currently paying.

They might be paying in terms of time, in terms of money, or most likely both.

What we also want to find out is the frequency of those time or money payments.

One of my favorite tools to use during interviewing is a pain and frequency matrix. (This is covered in more depth in Chapter 49, so I will only briefly mention it here.)

The idea is to map all of the problems you hear on a two-by-two grid of pain and frequency. Problems that are highly painful—lots of time, people, or steps involved—and high frequency are our prime fishing groups for product ideas.

Low frequency/high pain can be a good quadrant (like buying a house) as can high frequency/low pain (conventional "pain killers"). But you should avoid low pain/low frequency problems.

In the same way that you apply this to the overall problem selection process, you also want to apply this to thinking about pricing and pulling out information out about how much someone might be willing to pay.

Let's work through some examples.

Person: [describing a tool they use for the part of the process you solve]

You: Can I ask how much you pay for that?

Person: [amount]

You: And is that monthly, yearly, as you use it...?

It gets a little more complicated when your product solves multiple steps of a process that people currently use multiple tools for. (Remember, this includes manual tools). But it's worth dealing with this complication, because solving multiple steps can be a gold mine.

In that case, we would want to break down the individual steps and see how much time/money is spent on each one.

For example, let's say you're creating a no-code automation tool that helps university alumni departments figure out which cities to hold fundraising events in.

Context: "No-code" is a category of software tools that do not require the maker to use traditional programming languages and make it possible for people without a software engineering background to create digital products. Instead of directly interacting with servers and databases, they are built off of platforms like Bubble, Airtable, and spreadsheets. See makerpad.co for more on building a no-code business.

The following is an amalgamation of several different interviews I've had with customers.

Person: ...So first I get the online fundraising data for each donor in the last five years from our payment processor, and then I put it in Excel, then upload it to a tool to normalize the addresses and add the metropolitan statistical areas to find the nearest major city, and then I make a pivot table to see which cities we get the most money from, and then I pull in another spreadsheet with where we've held fundraising events the last year and how much we got from those events, and then I see which cities have the highest online donations but we haven't held any events in, and then that's the list I give to my manager for us to figure out where to hold the events.

Interviewer: Okay, wow, that sounds like a lot of work. I'd like to break it down a little. Can you tell me how long it takes you to get the data from the payment processor?

Person: Well, I have to pull the right data, and sometimes I have to change the export a little because it doesn't save my settings so I end up having to do the download a couple of times, so maybe half an hour. I also have to use a physical two-factor key to log into it, and I admit sometimes I sorta lose it in my desk drawer. (laughs) That's probably the most time consuming part.

Interviewer: Hah, okay, that makes sense. And the step to normalize the data and add the major cities, how long does that take?

Person: From the time I go to the website to when I can download the data, about fifteen minutes.

Interviewer: Wow, okay, sounds like that part is fast. How much does that cost?

Person: Usually about fifteen dollars I think?

Interviewer: And is that monthly, or one-time, or…

Person: It's just whenever I need it.

Interviewer: Okay, gotcha. Moving on to the part to create the pivot tables and bring in the data about the in-person fundraising events?

Person: Gosh I don't know, two days, maybe three? I have to get that fundraising data from another system, and it can be tricky sometimes. The formulas never seem to line up the same way, so I can kinda use my spreadsheet from last time but not really.

Interviewer: Oh, so it sounds like this analysis is something you've had to do multiple times?

Person: Yeah, we do it every year as part of our planning process.

Interviewer: Gotcha. So you said it can take a day or two to create that final list.

Person: Well, gosh, honestly maybe even a week sometimes! It's just so finicky. I have to get the data from that other system, and I can't get a spreadsheet, only a PDF printout, so I end up having to enter it all myself. And often times I need help using it, so I have to chase down someone in another department to help me. But you know, it's worth it.

Interviewer: Just out of curiosity, if you can tell me, how much do these new city events bring in in any given year?

Person: About two to three million dollars in a given year. They're a big part of meeting our fundraising goals.

ANALYSIS

So from a pain and frequency perspective with an eye toward price, what did we learn here?

- The person uses a combination of manual tools, in-house software, Excel, and external software
- The only tool they currently pay for with money for this specific process is the external software (Geocodio in this case), which is fifteen dollars
- This is a low-frequency, high-pain activity. It happens once a year but takes a week
- It's a high-payoff, critical activity that nets the department an additional two to three million dollars in fundraising revenue per year

If we add up the time spent:

- Gathering the initial data: thirty minutes
- Uploading the data: fifteen minutes
- Combining the data and doing the analysis: a week

If we add up money spent:

- Gathering the initial data: free
- Uploading the data: fifteen dollars
- Combining the data and doing the analysis: free

They aren't paying for a lot of services, yet it's very expensive in terms of time. Looking at the payoff and the cost of getting it wrong, there's a reasonable chance they'd pay for something that could connect all of that software. If your no-code automation tool could allow them to set this up once and then get the analysis back within thirty minutes, you can probably charge a good price for that on an annual recurring billing cycle (since this is an annual task).

THE QUESTIONS TO ASK

The next time you want to figure out how much someone would pay for something, here are the questions to ask.

Note that when you're asking about what people pay for things, you want to be extra polite. Say, "Can I ask..." rather than "What do..."

Depending on your cultural and professional context, it may not be possible to ask about specific costs. If that's the case, ask about the tools they use and other details that would help you figure out which plan they're using, pricing level, and so forth.

1. Can I ask what you're currently paying for that [tool] you mentioned?

2. And can I ask how often you pay that?

3. Could you tell me how long [particular step] takes you?

4. Can I ask how often you have to do that?

5. If you didn't do this [task], what would happen?

I suggest keeping an eye out for the high-pain, high-frequency problems.

Once you've decided on a problem, these questions will tell you what kind of billing model would match their usage frequency (usage-based versus subscription versus some combination). People will rarely pay for an annual subscription for a product they only need once a year.

Determining the final price will involve more work on your end—pricing is one of the most complicated parts of having a business in my opinion—but finding those high-pain/high-frequency problems and nailing the billing model to match the customer's mental model of the activity is the first step.

One of my favorite pricing guides is Patrick McKenzie's "Pricing Low-Touch SaaS." deployempathy.com/pricing

---

[47]

DEBUGGING INTERVIEWS

Every interview is an adventure in its own right.

You might walk into it hoping to find one thing and end up learning something completely different that you've never come across. (This is genuinely one of my favorite parts about it.)

But sometimes they're an adventure for reasons that aren't so exciting.

You get one-word responses. A person is rude. They tell you they only have ten minutes when you'd scheduled thirty. They talk about something that's entirely unrelated to what you hoped to hear about. You get a no-show.

This happens, and I want you to know that it's expected that things will go a little sideways sometimes. That's okay, and it isn't a reflection on your own skills.

Like programming, debugging is part of the process. Even the most experienced developers have bugs.

The difference is not the existence of bugs—it's how you handle them.

This is intended to help you overcome some common bugs in interviews, as something you can refer to when things don't go as you hoped or expected.

NO-SHOWS

This is far and away the most common interview problem: no-shows.

When I worked in a larger company, about ten percent of interviewees wouldn't show up. That was despite multiple confirmation emails *and* a twenty five dollar Amazon gift card.

I've found that my no-show rate went down significantly once I started recruiting personally and including my title in the email. As Cindy Alvarez says in *Lean Customer Development*, "It's harder to disappoint a known individual than a faceless user research recruiter."[1] When you send out bulk emails to recruit for interviews, make sure to include your title in the email.

In general, I find that interviews with non-users (whether phone or screen share) have the highest no-show rate.

The interviews with the lowest no-show rates are the ones that come out of customer support—usually when someone requests a feature or in reply to a one-question survey they've taken. Establishing even a tiny amount of rapport ahead of time goes a long way.

What to do when you get a no-show

- Give them fifteen minutes. Sometimes people get tied up or they forget. It's frustrating yet it happens. Give them fifteen minutes to get on the call, and if they don't, send them an email asking to reschedule:
- *Hi, I have it on my calendar that we were supposed to talk about [X] today at [time]. I'm gathering that something came up. Would another time be better? [calendar link]*
- Remember to send out calendar invites. Prevention is the best medicine. Always send out calendar invites with the call-in information and a ten-minute pre-meeting reminder.

INTERVIEWS ARE SHORTER THAN EXPECTED

Let's say you've planned for a half an hour interview but find both sides are running out of things to say after ten minutes.

This is something my *Software Social* podcast co-host Colleen Schnettler was running into. She'd go in with a script, all jazzed to talk, and then it would end up being over quickly.

Colleen realized it was because she was getting excited that she was solving the problem they experienced. She would start relating to them about the problem—a fairly common thing to do in a typical conversation—instead of diving deeper into how they experienced that problem and why, which is what you want to do in an interview.

This is common, especially when the person is describing a problem you're already familiar with. You may not feel the need to ask for further details.

Yet the goal is to figure out how this happens from their perspective, which can only be learned by asking them.

It takes time to adjust to asking for details about things you're already familiar with. Most educational systems and workplaces punish this kind of question-asking, so it makes sense if it feels like a strange concept to you.

It can also be a combination of setting an environment for listening and providing follow-ups. Follow-ups don't necessarily need to be questions. Some of the best follow-ups you can say are simple phrases.

What to do when your interviews are too short

- Mirroring and summarizing. This can be as simple as repeating back what the person has said. For example, if someone tells you they had issues with their database, you can say "It sounds like you had issues with the database?" and wait.
- *Can you say more about that?*
- Simple phrases that show you're listening, like "Mhmm," and "I see"

THE PERSON SEEMS NERVOUS

It's not uncommon to have someone be somewhat nervous.

Especially if you're doing a screen share test, someone might be worried that they're doing things wrong.

At the beginning of every screen share test, it's important to say, "We're just testing the website. It's still in early development so we know there are a lot of snags with it. The more honest you can be, the more you'll help us find those things. You can't do anything wrong."

What to do when the interviewee seems nervous

Validating statements. "That makes sense" and "I can see why you'd do it that way" go such a long way to reassure someone who is feeling nervous about sharing their experiences.

- Picture yourself as the rubber duck who is there to get more details, even if you already understand what they're doing (because you may not understand *why*). (See Chapter 37.)
- Remember to use your most harmless voice possible. A follow-up like "Oh, how interesting" can be taken very differently depending on the tone of voice. Remember to speak like you're talking to a respected grandparent. (See Chapter 25.)

THE PERSON IS GIVING SHORT ANSWERS

Perhaps you're asking questions about their overall goals and process and instead of getting the detail you'd hoped for, you're getting very short answers back said in a hurried or clipped tone. For example:

You: So can you tell me more about how you get the data into your CRM?

Person: I just upload it and then it's done.

You: Oh, okay. Can you say more?

Person: Nope that's it! What other questions do you have?

This can happen for a variety of reasons and doesn't necessarily mean you're doing something wrong.

Perhaps they've had something come up, and maybe they're pressed for time. (Asking, "Is now still a good time to talk?" is a good way to catch this in the beginning.)

Or maybe they took the call out of obligation and don't feel like they have much to say.

It's okay to cut it short if they don't have time or find another time to talk to them. People have last-minute things come up, they have emergencies, they forget about calls. It might be annoying for you to have this happen if you've made time for the call, yet we have to give people grace and remember that this happens. It's okay.

What to do when the interviewee gives short answers

- Check in with them. Say, "From the way you're responding, I'm getting the sense you might be in a time crunch. Would another time be better?"
- Ask if you should talk to someone else in the organization. "I really appreciate you taking the time to talk to me today. I'd like to learn about how [their company] does [X] from multiple perspectives. Is there anyone else you think I should talk to?"

THE PERSON IS BEING CAGEY

It's worth distinguishing between someone who is pressed for time and someone who is being cagey.

Perhaps they're giving answers that are evasive and encourage you to fill in the details. For example:

You: So can you tell me more about how you get the data into your CRM?

Person: Oh, I just put it in. You know how it works.

You: I'd like to hear more about how it works in your specific process.

Person: It's pretty simple. I just do it.

I've found that when this happens, it usually turns out that there are some misaligned expectations. Usually, it's that the person expected to get some onboarding help or wanted to request a feature. If that happens, it's okay to accept that this will not be an interview and pivot the conversation. (I cover those cases below.)

It can also be the case that they're working in an organization that is wary of sharing information about its processes and work.

Very rarely, it turns out that the person had widely different motives. I've had customers ask if we were planning to take funding, are interested in exiting, or otherwise had business-level questions (rather than product-level) that weren't exactly what we planned to discuss. Depending on your company goals and situation, this might be a welcome pivot (or not).

What to do when the interviewee is being cagey

- Check in with them. When this happens, I find it helpful to step back and see what their intentions are. In a very casual and curious tone, say, "You know, just to step back for a moment, I'm just curious. What made you interested in talking to me today?"
- If you get the sense that the evasiveness is because of privacy but could be overcome, ask if a nondisclosure agreement would help. "I understand this might be sensitive information. Would it be helpful if I signed an NDA?"

THE PERSON JUST WANTS TO TALK ABOUT FEATURE REQUESTS

Let's say you start out your interview like this:

You: Thank you for taking the time to talk to me. I really appreciate it. I have a handful of questions for you. Before I get started, I'm just wondering if you have any questions for me?

Them: Actually, yes. Have you guys considered adding support for [X]? And I'd love to be able to do [Y]. Are those on your roadmap?

It sounds like this person has some burning questions and this was their primary motivation for taking the call.

You should respect that and give them the space to get their questions answered. If you try to move them to the end of the call, the person may build up apprehension or frustration that their questions aren't being answered, and it could reduce the overall quality of answers you get back.

In this case, remember the skills you've learned to ask questions rather than give answers.

What to do when the interviewee just wants to share feature requests

When someone requests a feature, you can say something like, "We've had a few other people ask about that. I'm curious, could you tell me more about a situation when you'd use that?" and go into your typical feature request questions:

- "What do you currently use for this?"
- "How long does this currently take you to do this?"
- "How much do you currently pay to get this done?"

Going forward, you may also want to take a look at your recruiting copy. Having the opportunity to ask for feature requests is usually a great incentive for existing customers, yet you want to make it clear you'll have your own questions too.

THEY EXPECTED ONBOARDING

Another source of misaligned expectations comes from onboarding. I've generally found that this happens when the call happens too close to someone signing up.

Interviewer: Thank you for taking the time to talk to me. I really appreciate it. I have a handful of questions for you. Before I get started, I'm just wondering if you have any questions for me?

Person: Yeah. So how do I create an API key?

The first step here is to pull yourself back, recognize that you won't be able to jump into your script, and answer their questions.

If you don't, they might build up apprehension about whether they'll get their questions answered. They might give you shorter or less-detailed answers in an effort to rush through your questions to get to their own.

By putting their questions first, you can still get to your questions, but you may have to take a circuitous route there.

However, this isn't necessarily a bad thing. Especially in the early days of a product, getting details about any issues people are having getting started, what their projects are, and why they were looking to try something new are so incredibly helpful.

If you find a pattern of people continually wanting onboarding during your interview calls, consider moving the interviews back a bit. (Or whether your product needs more onboarding help. Perhaps your customers would pay extra for concierge onboarding, or you could do some usability testing via screen share to figure out what is causing common snags.)

There is a time and place for onboarding calls, and consider whether that is what you need right now. If you are having trouble activating users, you might want to talk to people within the first week before they forget about it.

What to do when the interviewee wants product help

- Be flexible. You hoped for one topic and got another. You may find it helpful to create an onboarding script for yourself as a back-up in case this happens. A good place to start is, "So tell me how it's going as you get started with [X]."

- Like when they come in expecting to talk about feature requests, look at your recruiting copy and timing. From my experience, interviews are best scheduled at least a month out from when someone has started using a product. Anything sooner tends to get interpreted as onboarding.

MULTIPLE PEOPLE ARE ON THE CALL FROM THEIR SIDE

Another issue can come up when it turns out that multiple team members are on a call. You may get a hunch about this in advance by seeing people confirm a forwarded event invitation, or it could be a surprise.

Interviewer: Hi, is this Owen?

Person: Yes, and I've also got Asuka, Marcus, and Deepak here.

Unfortunately, it's impossible to truly interview in a group setting.

Focus groups are helpful for seeing how people behave and make decisions in a group setting. If your product is generally sold to groups, this could be a good opportunity for you to learn about their decision-making process, roles, and interactions with other decision makers.

However, it will not give you the kind of process-level depth that you'd get from talking to one person alone. And since they're in a group setting, people may censor themselves or be less open than they would be in a 1-on-1 setting. Also, all of the relevant stakeholders for the decision-making process may not be in the room. It's a tricky situation.

What to do when multiple people show up

- Check in with them first. If this happens, check in with them immediately. Say, "Wow, thank you so much everyone for taking the time to hop on this call. I had some things I was wondering about from my perspective, but let's start out with you all. I'm interested to hear more about what led you to want to jump on today."

Usually, it turns out that they were hoping for training or some sort of onboarding help.

If group-level dynamics are helpful for you to understand, feel free to jump in. Just make sure you address their questions/motivations first.

THEY'RE TALKING ABOUT SOMETHING UNRELATED

Maybe you're having the opposite problem of short answers, and you're getting really long answers with lots of unrelated details.

I've had people start telling me about their cats, about their upcoming vacation, about all kinds of things.

Thankfully, that doesn't happen often, and it's more likely they start talking about an entirely unrelated process. Perhaps they start talking a lot about invoices when you'd hoped to hear about event planning.

This can be interesting, though. Because maybe it turns out your conceptualization of a problem is missing pieces, or there are adjacent steps that are far more painful than the problem you're intending to solve.

What to do when the interview goes off track

- Check in with yourself. Is what they're talking about completely unrelated (you asked about invoices and ten minutes later they're talking about cats) or related in a helpful way (you asked about invoices and they're talking about difficulties with vendor coordination)? It could be that you've uncovered an even bigger problem for them.
- Polite re-steering. "Thank you for telling me that. That makes sense. I'm wondering if we could go back to something you mentioned earlier. Could you tell me more about how you use [something on-topic]?"

It's also possible you've uncovered something that is important to this person that no one else has ever asked about. As a human, that's an important moment. It builds trust and affinity. Sometimes it's worth letting someone go on a bit about an unrelated topic to build rapport. The more you do interviews, the more you'll get a hang for when you should dive deeper versus when you should re-steer the conversation.

THEY'RE MAD ABOUT SOMETHING

This is a very rare occurrence in my experience (maybe one or two in the thousands of interviews I've done across consumer and business settings), and it receives an outsized amount of nervousness among new interviewers, so I would be remiss not to mention it.

You: Hi, is this Joe?

Person (gruff): Yeah.

You: Thank you for taking the time to talk to me. I have a few questions for you. Before we get started, do you have any questions for me?

Person: Yeah, why'd you charge my credit card $$$? What kind of service is this even?

The first thing to do when someone is mad is to listen to them and let them get it out.

Nothing can happen until they have aired their grievances and felt heard.

Next, you can determine whether this problem is solvable, and work toward a solution for this.

If you're able to calm them down, it would be incredibly valuable to you to figure out why they signed up for your product in the first place. Do you have a landing page that sounded like it solved their problem when you solve something completely different? Are you accidentally running ads on unrelated keywords? After they feel heard, try to walk through what happened from their perspective to figure out the source of the misunderstanding.

Whether it was an unexpected charge, a feature that didn't work the way they wanted it to, or some other experience that didn't go as they'd expected... whatever it may be, try to get there.

Pivoting to their own sense of generosity sometimes helps. "This has been a really frustrating situation for you, and we'd like to use this as a chance to make sure no one else has this same experience you've had. Would you be able to tell me more about what you were trying to do in the first place and how you came across us?"

What to do if the interviewee is mad about something

- Listen. Listen, listen, listen. People who are angry first need to feel heard. Resist the urge to defend yourself or your product.
- Establish your competence. "I can help you sort this out" is a helpful phrase to use here.
- Solve *their* problem. If you can, do it while they're on the phone. Give them a refund, close their account. Angry former customers with unsolved problems are very expensive for a company that relies on word of mouth.
- Solve *your* problem. Try to get to the root of where the misunderstanding came from.

[PART 8]
ANALYZING INTERVIEWS

Interviews can lead to actions for:

- Marketing
- Figuring out what to build in the first place
- Long-term strategic decision making
- Pricing decisions
- Customer acquisition flow design
- Prioritizing new features
- Business development
- And more

What you apply the learnings from interviews for at the current moment is up to you.

This chapter introduces two different analysis methods:

- Using transcripts to create a simple customer journey map
- Using the Pain and Frequency Matrix to identify high pain, high frequency problems that are underserved by current solutions

You might find it helpful to sketch the customer's process or pain and frequency during the interview, or right after. However, you should never make business decisions after one interview.

It can be hard to draw the line between when you jump to action and when you wait. It can be hard to put something off when you think you've identified a problem.

I'll never forget a round of usability testing I did years ago when I was first learning about user research. A user had tremendous confusion with the arrangement of some buttons, and we sprang to action and changed them before the next session... only to introduce bugs that the next person ran into (and to discover that the next person found the new arrangement confusing). It muddled our data.

If there were a Murphy's Law of Websites, it would say that typos and broken links will only make themselves known when someone else is looking at the site. So those are fair game for immediate fixes. I do urge you to contain yourself from making any larger, even if minor, changes before talking to five people. (See Chapter 16, How Many People Should You Talk To? for more on this.)

Once you have done an interview and analyzed it, you have created a permanent resource for the company. Even if you don't act on all of it now, you can reference it in years to come as new questions come up.

[48]

DRAWING A SIMPLE CUSTOMER JOURNEY MAP

If you've recorded your interviews, it can be both helpful and time saving to get them transcribed. There are a variety of AI tools that make transcription affordable and fast now. I personally use Otter.ai.

After you get the transcript back, you can read through it, highlighter in hand, and pull out key parts and phrases. You will want to pay attention to the core questions, functional/social/emotional dimensions, tools/processes used, as well as the specific phrasing and wording they use to describe those steps and struggles.

Core Questions

- What are they trying to do overall?
- What are all of the steps in that process?
- Where are they now?
- Where does the problem you are solving fit in that process?
- Where in that process do they spend a lot of time or money?
- What have they already tried?

I suggest drawing a simple version of a customer journey map,[1] which is a tool widely used by user researchers. The goal is to be able to draw out the different steps a customer goes through, and then for each step, identify the functional/social/emotional elements. It can also be helpful to diagram the different tools and constraints that might exist at a particular step. It may not be linear, and it may have branches.

You can also consider visualizing it in a spreadsheet or database. For example, if you were drawing a table:

[Overall Process/Activity]

	Step 1	Step 2	Step 3	...
Functional				
Social				
Emotional				
Quote				

How you store and save this information can vary widely from person to person and company to company. This might include:

- Visualizing their entire process in a spreadsheet, separated by the functional/social/elements at each step
- Pulling out key phrases and attaching them to a story for a particular landing page, feature, or project

George Stocker, a technology change management consultant, makes transcripts and then compares them from interview to interview. That helps him "see the common trends when doing client research for consulting [and see] what jargon is used most, which words get repeated the most across interviews, and understand how different clients respond to the same question." George also uses Otter.ai and appreciates the summary of key phrases included at the top of their transcript exports, which makes it easy to find important words.

At Stripe, there is not one formal codified analysis process, and teams can approach analysis as a collaborative process. According to Stripe product manager Theodora Chu, here is how her teams have analyzed their user interviews:[2]

1. Pull together everyone's notes from the interviews.

2. Hold a review session among the people who did the interviews. In the session, everyone reads through the transcripts and notes.

3. Next, they pull out themes, with specific quotes from users. At this point, themes are not pulled with any eye towards actions or impact—simply all of the themes the team can find are pulled out and organized.

4. Intentionally "sit on the themes for a little bit" and give everyone a chance to think about the themes.

5. Schedule a second session and brainstorm what the actions might be and what they will recommend. Those recommendations may be for their roadmap, strategy, or a particular feature.

6. Share the themes and proposed actions with leadership.

[49]

THE PAIN AND FREQUENCY MATRIX

The more frequent and painful a problem is, the more likely someone will be willing to pay to solve it.

That's the underlying idea of the pain and frequency Matrix. It's based on a matrix promoted by Des Traynor, cofounder of customer support software company Intercom and Jobs To Be Done advocate.[1]

"For many products the problem isn't the quality, it's the priority of the problem in the customer's lives. If your potential customers don't care about solving their problem, it's a good sign you shouldn't either... Ultimately, you can succeed as a product but still fail as a business if you find yourself in this trap."[2]

Traynor graphs problems by size versus frequency, but I prefer to use "pain." I generally call it the pain and frequency matrix, and you can also think about it as a complexity and frequency, or time and frequency matrix, whichever clicks with you.

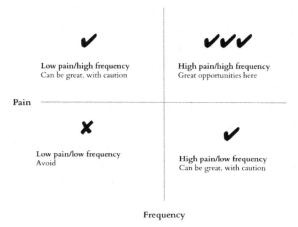

For this matrix, you can chart both huge activities (buying a house), smaller activities, and even individual tasks. Let's work through a few examples.

- **Buying a house**. The average American buys three houses in their lifetime. This is therefore an infrequent problem and will fall on the bottom part of the matrix. Buying a house is also an extremely complicated process with a lot of steps that are extremely expensive to get wrong (from names being wrong on the deed to missing a critical structural problem). Because of that complexity and the cost of getting the complexity wrong, people therefore pay a lot of money to buy a house. Buying a house would then be in the low-frequency, high-pain category.
- **Making a transcript of a podcast**. Every week, we release a new episode of *Software Social*, and it's important to us that the podcast is released with a transcript for both marketing and accessibility reasons. The weekly need makes this a high-frequency problem. Making the transcript manually, however, can be incredibly time-consuming. I did it for our first few episodes and it took me about an hour and a half for a half-hour podcast. This puts it in the high pain

category. When a friend told me about Otter.ai, which can automatically create transcripts in about ten minutes, it seemed obvious to pay eight dollars a month to save myself that time-consuming manual transcription time.

- **Scheduling a meeting.** You've probably been on email threads back and forth about finding a mutually agreeable time for a phone call. For the average business person, this is a fairly common problem, putting it in the high frequency category. Scheduling isn't necessarily painful but it is annoying and does take up a few minutes, meaning this is, for the average person, in the low-pain category. This would then be high frequency, low pain.

It's worth noting that each one of the above examples can change based on context—both the person's situation and the different functional, social, and emotional factors that play into their decision-making. For example, a salesperson who is incentivized to hold client meetings may schedule a lot of meetings across different time zones, making it a higher-frequency, higher-pain problem (due to the sheer number of meetings). A massage therapist might also schedule a lot of meetings, but have different social, emotional, and functional contexts. That context leads people to need different features, and fundamentally the question the matrix helps solve is, "Which customer contexts have the highest frequency problems that are the most aligned with my internal capabilities and opportunities?"

I encourage you to use it in tandem with Marty Cagan's viable, valuable, feasible, usable framework (see Chapter 9). There are many high-frequency, high-pain problems in the world, but not all of them can be solved with your own abilities or make sense from a competitive standpoint.

Within or after an interview, you might diagram the different steps you heard in the interview. For example, in the sample interview, "selecting a database" was an infrequent problem (only done once), while "users uploading files" was a high-frequency problem (may happen multiple times per day).

PRACTICE THIS NOW

Grab a piece of paper and a pencil. Draw a two-by-two grid, and label one axis with Pain and the other with Frequency. Then, plot the following tasks:

- Doing laundry
- Filing taxes
- Making coffee or tea in the morning

Now, dive into the steps that go into one of those tasks and plot each individual step. For example, laundry:

- Sorting laundry into lights, colors, and delicates
- Figuring out what the laundry care symbols on garments mean
- Putting away laundry in drawers
- Hanging up clothing
- Switching a load from the washer to the dryer
- Selecting and measuring the right kind of soap
- Line-drying sweaters and delicates
- Cleaning the lint filter
- Removing a stain

In the first exercise, I'm willing to bet your sense of time was more expansive. Filing taxes only happens once a year, so perhaps your mental sense for the maximum time was a year, with filing taxes going in the "low-frequency, high-pain" category.

In the second, you're looking at a task itself that happens much more frequently. The longest tasks might be putting away laundry (which can take a few hours), so perhaps that was the upper limit for time in this case.

Time and complexity are all relative.

It's also worth noting that one overarching task can be very different from person to person and organization to organization, and is also context-dependent.

Coffee is a particularly fun example because it can differ widely from person to person, or even day-to-day based on how much time someone has. People might have a variety of situational substitutes based on different conditions they may be under and the different functional, social, and emotional dimensions present.

For example, "making coffee" could be:

1. Locate a mug.
2. Select a Keurig pod.
3. Put the pod in the machine.
4. Put the cup in the machine.
5. Press down the handle.
6. Take coffee from the machine
7. Drink coffee

Now let's look at another way of making coffee:

1. Select beans
2. Determine the right amount of beans to use
3. Measure out the right amount of beans
4. Grind the beans
5. Boil water
6. Place the dripper on top of a carafe
7. Put a filter into the top of dripper
8. Wet the filter in the dripper
9. Pour the ground coffee into the dripper
10. Place the apparatus on a kitchen scale and zero the scale
11. Determine the right amount of water to pour
12. Pour water
13. Let sit for the desired amount of time
14. Locate a mug
15. Pour into a mug
16. Drink coffee

The same person might choose to use a pod machine during the week when they are pressed for time (*emotional*) and only need one cup in their to-go container (*functional*) to drink while they drive to work alone in their car (*social*). But the same person may choose to do Chemex on the weekend when they have guests over (*social*) and need to make a large batch (*functional*) and want to impress their friends (*emotional*). That same person may buy the fancy Chemex with the *intent* to use it when they have guests over and never actually use it, but the reason why they bought is still tied back to the functional, social, and emotional dimensions that they're picturing as they hold the product in the store.

USING THIS TO ANALYZE INTERVIEWS

As I do an interview, I build a mental model of how they approached something. The scaffolding of this model is:

1. All of the individual steps
2. The pain/complexity/time involved in each step
3. The frequency of each step (Does this step happen every time? Just sometimes? Just once? How often?)

When someone is describing a process, you want to use the pain and frequency matrix from two perspectives. I suggest using a different piece of paper for each of these:

1. To compare different processes to one another (filing taxes versus doing laundry)
2. To granularly understand the complexity of each step

I suggest looking at the customer's problem set both linearly as a step-by-step process, and also as a matrix. Using those tools together can help give you a more complete picture of what the problem/s is/are and how critical they are to a customer.

If you want to go one step further and validate your guesses about the complexity of problems, you could do card sorting interviews with customers. See Chapter 44.

WHAT THIS MODEL TELLS YOU (AND WHAT IT DOESN'T)

The pain and frequency matrix will tell you what problems are frequent and painful for people and are thus the things they're most likely to be willing to buy.

I also want to make it clear what this model won't tell you. It won't tell you specifically how to get to market, how to sell, which exact price to choose, or any of those other things that are key to building a product. (Your interviews will give you clues toward those things.)

What the pain and frequency matrix will tell you is which problems are the most acute. That can help you weed through the many different possible problems you could pursue, what should be prioritized on your roadmap, or which problems you should abandon.

Try this now
To start, try to notice how often you do particular tasks, and how much they annoy you or have complexity. Try to get used to working with it in your daily life, and then apply it to how you think about business.

[PART 9]
PULLING IT ALL TOGETHER: SAMPLE INTERVIEW

Maybe you're starting out here, or maybe you're ending here.

However you want to work this sample interview into your learning process is okay. I trust you to know when an example would be helpful for you.

In the dozens of interviews I conducted with early readers of this book, this sample interview was consistently named one of the most helpful and unique parts of this book.

You will only get a small portion of the benefit by reading the transcript, so I encourage you to find time to listen to the interview. You can find it at deployempathy.com/sample-interview.

This interview was conducted in March 2021 for my podcast, *Software Social*. We discussed my cohost's product, Simple File Upload, which he had recently started using. Accordingly, the interview follows the Switch Interview Script.

I didn't previously have any conversations with the participant, Drew, so what you are reading is a genuine example of a customer interview.

Note: The interview is with a developer and contains a fair amount of technical product names and terms. It's okay if you don't recognize all of them. The point is to notice how the questions are asked, the answers they receive, and the pacing.

If you are curious, I've explained some of the terms in the endnotes.

[50]
SAMPLE INTERVIEW TRANSCRIPT

Michele: Hi, Is this Drew?

Drew: Yep, this is Drew.

Michele: Hi, Drew. Thank you so much for taking the time to talk to me today. I really appreciate it.

Drew: Not a problem. Thank you for having me.

Michele: So before we get started, I just want to ask if you had any questions for me?

Drew: Not off the top of my head. I'm sure I'll find some along the way.

Michele: Okay, feel free to ask any questions that might come up.

Drew: Okay.

Michele: And just before we get started, I just want to make sure that it's okay if we record this interview.

Drew: Yeah, absolutely.

Michele: Okay, so just to get started, could you just tell me a little bit about how you came to even needing something like Simple File Upload in the first place?

Drew: I'm building a product that is a job listing platform.[1] We wanted companies to be able to upload their logo to sit next to their listing.[2] But for our stage two of that, we're actually adding in some more verbose user accounts, where users will have avatars. They'll be able to upload resumes and stuff like that.[3]

So we just really saw that we were gonna need something that would allow us to upload all the files and handle them easily.[4]

Michele: Yeah, that makes sense. I'm curious, have you tried anything else to do this?

Drew: Yeah, we were using Firebase Storage,[5] because we were using Firestore as our database.[6] So we started using Firebase Storage just because, you know, they were right next to each other [and it] seemed like an easy enough fit.[7] And it was working at first.

But we recently started going through a big migration to Next.js,[8] [where] some things are just handled a little differently from a code perspective. And Firebase Storage just did not work as easily as it was supposed to. We found ourselves running into a lot of walls, jumping through a lot of hoops just to make the simplest things work.

Michele: Can you tell me a little bit more about those hoops and walls that you ran into?[9]

Drew: I'm trying to think of a specific case.[10] So we're really just trying to load the image before the component was loaded so it would be there when the page did load.[11] But because of how they give you access to it, with promises, and all of that fun stuff, I don't know if it's because we were implementing it wrong, or maybe they just weren't ever really meant to work hand in hand, but we were getting errors that it couldn't do what we were asking because the data it needed wasn't there yet when it was asking for it. And we really started to feel like we were just putting Band-Aids on things to make something work, and this was really kind of our big push to make the platform more stable, not less. That was probably the biggest one.

Michele: Sounds like that was frustrating. A lot of fits and starts for you guys.[12]

Drew: Yeah, it really was because we had it working, and it took a little bit of work to get it working that first time. And most every other piece of the code kind of just transferred one-to-one for the most part, and this part just did not. And we already had a decent amount of files in the storage that we wanted to get to, but for what-ever reason, be it user error or storage error, it just wasn't happening.

Michele: Yeah, do you remember how long it was from the time when you decided to start using Firebase Storage? And then until you decided it wasn't going to work? How long was that?[13]

Drew: Oh, we started using it around a year ago, and it was working fine. We started working on this big rebuild about maybe a month and a half ago, and that was probably when we started real-izing that it wasn't gonna work. And I think I spent probably three days trying to wrestle it before I just relented.

Michele: Oh, man. So it took six weeks of trying to get it to work, and then you intensely worked on it for three days, and then it still wouldn't work.[14]

Drew: Well, the six weeks wasn't fully working on trying to get it to work. Six weeks was getting all the components moved over, and all that other stuff set up for the new environment. But you are correct, it was three intense days of trying to make it work.

Michele: Man, that must have been super frustrating.[15]

Drew: It was, and I was at my wits' end.[16]

Michele: So when did you start thinking that maybe [you could] use something else?[17]

Drew: Almost immediately, I wanted to use something else, but I didn't know what else would be out there at the pricing model that they provide.[18] But I guess, free always comes with caveats, and I found those caveats early on.

Michele: Oh, so Firebase Storage was free if you were using Firestore.[19]

Drew: Yeah, they have this whole platform set up where it's free up until X amount of requests, but that number is really high. So it's really enticing when you just want to get something up and moving. We just kept hitting brick walls with the storage.

Michele: Yeah, it sounds like it. So, you had three days of intensely trying to work on this. You wanted to use something else, but you didn't know what other options there were. Did you start researching other options? Can you walk me through that a little bit?[20]

Drew: I didn't really research too many options, just because the product we're building is not generating any revenue, and it's kind of a "side project last, first status." So I wasn't really seriously considering anything that had a paywall on it because I wasn't sure that it would ever pay itself back off. I knew there were other options out there that would either require moving our storage and our database altogether, which didn't really seem appealing, or having two different services, one to manage each, but then the storage still being just as complicated, only somewhere else.[21]

Michele: It sounds like you had a lot of things you were trying to weigh back and forth about whether you should sort of try to plunge forward with this thing that was already being very frustrating, and then all of the negative effects of switching and all the complications that would introduce.

Drew: Yeah, I really didn't want to spend a whole lot of time investing or building up a new infrastructure for a new product to handle this one thing. I think the most frustrating part was that it worked and now it doesn't.[22]

Michele: Yeah, that's such a letdown.[23] So, I just want to ask about something you said. You said you didn't want to consider anything with a paywall, and when you say paywall, do you mean something that has a free tier and then it goes to pay as you go? Or something that you have to pay for upfront? I'm just wondering if you can say what you meant by that.[24]

Drew: The other options that I knew were out there usually had [an] upfront paywall that—well, I guess not upfront paywall, it was kind of a pay-as-you-go, depending on what you use. And I didn't know what those numbers would equate to. So where we were in the project, I didn't want to invest too much mental overhead into trying to figure that out.[25] I really wanted to stay focused on just building the thing.

Michele: That makes sense. Yeah. So it sounds like the pricing models, based on what you were doing, it was unclear what you would have to pay for those if you had to pay for them.

Drew: Yeah, exactly.

Michele: And you just wanted to get this thing that you thought was gonna be easy out the door, and the thought of doing all those calculations was not really where your head was at.[26]

Drew: Yeah.

Michele: Yeah, that makes sense. So let's jump to Simple File Upload. Can you just let me know how you heard about it?

Drew: I heard about it through two different ways. I heard about it in a virtual coffee community I'm in. And then I also heard about it through the Twitterverse.

Michele: And so can you tell me when you first heard about it? Was this around the same time that you were trying to wrangle this whole Firebase thing? Or was it after? Or was it before?[27]

Drew: It was a little bit before. So I think I first heard about it when we were at the very beginning of the big framework migration. So it was kind of at the beginning of that when I heard about it, but at that point in time, our current solution worked. So I wasn't really, at that point, I wasn't really looking for anything else.

Michele: That makes sense. And then you had those sort of three days of struggle, and then it occurred to you at some point that you could maybe use Simple File Upload for that. Does that sound right?

Drew: Oh, no, it never occurred to me. I was gonna continue banging my head on the keyboard. But a friend in the virtual coffee community said, "Hey, why don't you just try this thing?" Because I'd already heard about it in the virtual coffee [community] and had already heard about it on Twitter. And at that point, I was so white knuckling to holding on to our current solution that the thought hadn't even registered. Yeah, so someone else recommended it. And as soon as they said it, I was like, this is it. I hope this works.

Michele: It sounds like you put so much work into trying to make the other thing work that you were like, really wanted that to work. You didn't want to have to walk away from all of that frustration that you went through.

Drew: Yeah, I did. I was being very stubborn.

Michele: That makes sense. I mean, it sounds like you poured a lot of effort into it. But then, so this friend that you heard about Simple File Upload from, had they used it themselves?

Drew: I'm not sure if they use it themselves. I know he and Colleen [Schnettler, the founder of Simple File Upload] both work with Ruby.[28] So maybe he was more familiar with it because they had chatted about it from that perspective.

Michele: You said you had heard about it through these groups you're in. Did you look for any other places for information about it before you decided to use it?[29]

Drew: I looked at the website and kind of skimmed the documentation and somehow came across a Code Pen[30] or some type of little code snippet that let me kind of test drive it. And based on that, I was like, if it's really this easy, then I don't see why I wouldn't use it.

Michele: So before you started using it, was there anything you were sort of [unsure about]? It sounds like you were unsure if it was actually as good as it seemed? Is there anything else that you were unsure about? Or you weren't able to figure out before you used it?

Drew: I don't want to say [I was] unsure of how the Amazon S3[31] buckets and stuff worked. I knew that's what it connected to and that's how it worked. But I've heard a bunch of people get frustrated about how complicated that would be. I guess I was curious as to whether or not it actually made it that simple.

Michele: It sounds like you were almost doubtful whether it could be that easy.[32]

Drew: Yeah, it seems like from what I've heard about S3 buckets, that that's such a big problem that it wouldn't necessarily be an easy thing to wrangle into a simple solution.

Michele: So have you gotten the chance to use it yet?

Drew: Oh, yeah.

Michele: Okay, so how did it go?

Drew: I think I had it working in five minutes.

Michele: And how did that make you feel?[33]

Drew: Oh, man, I was elated. If I didn't live in South Georgia, I would have shouted it from the mountaintops.

Michele: I think you still could.

Drew: Yeah, absolutely.

Michele: Wow. And so you were able to sort of drop it in where you previously were using the Firebase Storage?

Drew: Yep, I don't even really think there was much configuration needed. So I'm specifically using the React component version of it. So I just kind of got my account set up, dropped in the React component, and there, it really just worked.

Michele: And so it sounds like it's really working for you. And you had looked into some other things. And I'm curious, for the site you're working on, are you working on that with other people?[34]

Drew: Yeah, so there's a team of five of us. But we call it a "side project first priority, last thing" that we're working on. So there's five of us that work on it, but one of us may be full tilt for two weeks straight, and then you won't hear from us for a month or two.

Michele: Gotcha. So when you were sort of in that period of knowing that what you were doing wasn't going to work, even though that was sort of hard to admit to yourself, understandably, and then deciding to switch to Simple File Upload, was there anyone else you talked to about that decision within the team, or the company?[35]

Drew: I mentioned it. I mentioned it to everyone. I guess it was never really put to the table for a vote. But I was just kind of like, "Hey, we keep running into problems with this current thing. I'm going to give this a try and see what happens." And I think everyone on the team had already heard about Simple File Upload because they're in the same virtual coffee community. So I want to say it was a unanimous yes.

Michele: And was there anyone outside of the team who needed to weigh in on that, or anything like that?

Drew: Not really. Right now, it's a small project, small team.

Michele: Gotcha. So you've gotten to implement it. And so you have it working on the site now with the logos?[36]

Drew: Yep. It's working. It's up and working. And it's beautiful.

Michele: Yeah. So do you think you're going to use it for the applicant photos as well?

Drew: I believe so. Yeah. We have it working in this instance. Or we have it working in the way we need it now, so I can only see it making the other places we need file upload better.

Michele: Cool. Well, thank you so much for taking the time to talk to me. I've learned so much from you. Is there anything else you think I should know?[37]

Drew: I guess now that we've been talking about it, I do have a question — and this would probably end up being a feature request more than anything. But are there plans in the future to, from the Simple File Upload dashboard, to be able to section off different stuff? You know, maybe this is type A files vs type B? Or is that already there and I haven't seen it?

Michele: So I can't speak to that, because I don't work on it myself, but could you walk me through how that would fit into your process, or how that would help you?[38]

Drew: Sure. We're going to be rolling out some user accounts. There's gonna be two different types of accounts, and so one of the account types is going to have avatars and PDFs. It may or may not even be necessary, because at the end, all we just need is the URL anyways. But if for whatever reason we do need to go to the dashboard to see those files, it would be nice if they could be sectioned off. You know, "These are our user accounts. These are our company accounts."

Michele: Oh, got it. So the first one are the users, like people uploading resumes, is that right? And then the second one is the companies and then all the images associated with the companies.[39]

Drew: Yeah.

Michele: Which will be the logos.

Drew: Yeah. And that may not even be necessary, because we're really just taking the URL and piping it in somewhere.

Michele: Yeah. Could you just tell me a situation where you would need to [do that]? Distinguishing between those files, what would that help you do? What's a situation where that would be helpful?[40]

Drew: I can't think of one off the top of my head. But when we first started working towards getting user accounts in place, that was actually a question one of my team members brought up was, when we send this to Simple File Upload, do we have to specify that it goes to this file or this file, or is it all the same place? And it's kind of, "Oh, that's a good question."

Michele: And did that person want them to be differentiated?

Drew: I don't think they necessarily wanted them to be differentiated, as much as they were just making sure that they weren't doing it the wrong way by not specifying somewhere.

Michele: Gotcha. Gotcha. They wanted to make sure they were using the tool right?

Drew: Yeah.

Michele: Yeah. Yeah, that makes sense. You had mentioned with Firebase that you guys were kind of unsure whether it was user error, versus the limitations of the tool. And so it kind of makes sense that you would have questions about using it right.

Drew: Yeah, because we're mostly junior developers building this. So we're making it up as we go.

Michele: We all are.

Drew (Laughing)

Michele: Cool. Was there, or is there anything else? Did you have any other questions?

Drew: No, I think that's everything I have.

Michele: Okay, great. Well, thank you so much for taking the time to do this today. I really appreciate it.

Drew: Thank you. It was my pleasure.

Michele: All right. Thank you so much.

Drew: Thank you.

Michele: Bye.

51

SAMPLE ANALYSIS

You may pull different actions and questions from the sample interview, and that's okay. Everyone notices different things in interviews, and having someone else review your interviews will help you pull more out of them.

> Griffin and Hauser found that teams were more effective at pulling out user needs than individuals. Indeed, engineering teams pulled more user needs out of an interview than a qualitative research expert! However, don't let that discourage you if you're working alone. Pulling out 80 percent of the insights from an interview you've conducted and analyzed solo is better than zero percent from not doing the interview at all.

WHAT HE'S TRYING TO DO OVERALL AND WHERE THE PROBLEM THE PRODUCT SOLVES SITS

It's important to differentiate between the process someone is going through to accomplish a goal and the process they go through regarding deciding to use a specific product. I encourage you to break down the goal-level process first, then the product-level process.

For a new customer, the experience of switching to a new solution will be on the surface and may be easier to find. Talking to long-time customers may give you greater granularity on their overall process (at the expense of hearing about the decision process).

What are they trying to do overall? "I'm building a product that is a job listing platform."

What are the steps of that process and where does the problem you are solving fit in that process?

- "We wanted companies to be able to upload their logo to sit next to their listing. But for our stage two of that, we're actually adding in some more verbose user accounts, where users will have avatars. They'll be able to upload resumes and stuff like that. So we just really saw that we were gonna need something that would allow us to upload all the files and handle them easily."
- More granular: "trying to load the image before the component was loaded so it would be there when the page did load."

THE STEPS OF THE DECISION PROCESS, FROM TRYING SOMETHING ELSE, TO STRUGGLING, TO SWITCHING, TO BEING SATISFIED USING IT

For an interview with a relatively new customer, it can be illuminating to dive into their decision process for why they switched from one solution to another.

It may not be possible to build out this decision process for someone who has been happily using a product for a long time, and that's okay. (This is why it's good to talk to many different customers at different stages on a regular basis.)

Overall timeline: "We started using it around a year ago, and it was working fine. We started working on this big rebuild about maybe a month and a half ago, and that was probably when we started realizing that it wasn't gonna work. And I think I spent probably three days trying to wrestle it before I just relented."

1. For this specific problem, started with Firebase Storage because it was integrated with Firebase: "We were using Firebase Storage, because we were using Firestore as our database. So we started using Firebase Storage just because, you know, they were right next to each other [and it] seemed like an easy enough fit."

2. Heard about Simple File Upload but decided not to use it: "So I think I first heard about it when we were at the very beginning of the big framework migration. So it was kind of at the beginning of that when I heard about it, but at that point in time, our current solution worked. So I wasn't really, at that point, I wasn't really looking for anything else."

3. Broader context: Migrating underlying code to Next.js: "We recently started going through a big migration to Next.js, [where] some things are just handled a little differently from a code perspective. And Firebase Storage just did not work as easily as it was supposed to."

4. Migration to Next.js created unforeseen problems with Firebase Storage: "We had it working, and it took a little bit of work to get it working that first time. And most every other piece of the code kind of just transferred one-to-one for the most part, and this part just did not."

"We were getting errors that it couldn't do what we were asking because the data it needed wasn't there yet when it was asking for it. And we really started to feel like we were just putting Band-Aids on things to make something work, and this was really kind of our big push to make the platform more stable, not less."

5. Considered switching to something else, but didn't think there were any good options, so he kept trying to get it to work: "Almost immediately, I wanted to use something else, but I didn't know what else would be out there at the pricing model that they provide."

"I was so white knuckling to holding on to our current solution that the thought hadn't even registered."

"I was being very stubborn."

6. A friend reminded him about Simple File Upload (implied: he told a friend about the problem): "But a friend in the virtual coffee community said, 'Hey, why don't you just try this thing?'"

7. Brought up the issues and potential switch with his team: "I mentioned it. I mentioned it to everyone...But I was just kind of like, 'Hey, we keep running into problems with this current thing. I'm going to give this a try and see what happens.'"

8. He was a bit worn out and was unsure whether it would work: "I was at my wits' end."

"Someone else recommended [Simple File Upload]. And as soon as they said it, I was like, this is it. I hope this works."

"I've heard a bunch of people get frustrated about how complicated [S3 buckets are]. I guess I was curious as to whether or not it actually made it that simple."

9. Once he finally switched, it was easy and he was "elated": "I just kind of got my account set up, dropped in the React component, and there, it really just worked."

"I think I had it working in five minutes."

"I was elated."

10. Planning to use it for other elements of the product (another sign of satisfaction): "I can only see it making the other places we need file upload better."

THE INTELLECTUAL, SOCIAL, AND EMOTIONAL DIMENSIONS THAT INFLUENCED THE DECISION-MAKING AND HIS PRODUCT SATISFACTION

We may not like to admit it, but the reasons why we do and buy things go beyond their functional purposes. Emotions and social considerations are drivers, too.

Functional

- Upload images and files so they can use them on the job listing website; limited time for this project
- "[We] Need[ed] something that would allow us to upload all the files and handle them easily"
- "There's gonna be two different types of accounts, and so one of the account types is going to have avatars and PDFs"
- Limited time on the project: "We call it a "side project first priority, last thing" that we're working on. So there's five of us that work on it, but one of us may be full tilt for two weeks straight, and then you won't hear from us for a month or two."
- "I really didn't want to spend a whole lot of time investing or building up a new infrastructure for a new product to handle this one thing."

Emotional

- Thought it would be quick and easy; disappointment when it wasn't; nervous about switching to a new solution because of pricing and product uncertainties; elation when it worked
- "I really wanted to stay focused on just building the thing."
- Recurring theme about uncertainty about whether he was using a product wrong or something was wrong with the product
- "We're mostly junior developers building this. So we're making it up as we go."
- "I don't know if it's because we were implementing it wrong, or maybe they just weren't ever really meant to work hand in hand"

- "But for whatever reason, be it user error or storage error, it just wasn't happening"
- "Free always comes with caveats, and I found those caveats early on."
- "I was at my wits' end."

Social

- Working within a team setting; friend recommended switching to Simple File Upload; team discussion/decision about switching
- "There's a team of five of us"
- "A friend in the virtual coffee community said, 'Hey, why don't you just try this thing?'"
- "I think everyone on the team had already heard about Simple File Upload because they're in the same virtual coffee community. So I want to say it was a unanimous yes."
- Feature request came from a team member (and not someone in leadership): "That was actually a question one of my team members brought up"

PAIN, FREQUENCY, AND WILLINGNESS TO PAY

- Installing a file management service is a one-time task for a project but it can be painful to set up, especially for junior developers.
- This has implications for buyer personas and further research. Do large companies only install file management once, or do they use different products for different projects (as is happening in this case)? Do consultants use the same solution for different client projects? Need to do further

research to understand which buyers may be the best for
business goals.

- The underlying problem the product solves is frequent
  (users of the customer's website uploading resumes and
  logos in this case), which bodes well for a subscription
  product.
- File management is key to the success of the customer's
  product. Getting it wrong means that people on the job
  listing platform may not be able to upload their resumes
  (critical for usability) or companies wouldn't be able to
  upload their logos (critical for user growth from the
  company perspective).
- For this project, low willingness to pay before the product
  itself has proven itself and generates revenue. (This suggests
  exploring a freemium model, but that may not be *viable* for
  the business.)

52

QUICK ANALYSIS

Sometimes you may have time to pore through interview transcripts, highlight them, and collate the results. Copious examples of that process are available in other books on user research.[1]

Other times, you may want to do a faster analysis while it's still fresh. Since this book is intended for people who may be juggling many other things and may not have the kind of time that a full journey map would require, we will do an express analysis here.

IMMEDIATE ACTIONS

1. Make documentation and Code Pen accessible from homepage

- "I looked at the website and kind of skimmed the documentation and somehow came across a Code Pen or some type of little code snippet that let me kind of test drive it."
- **Action (marketing):** Put the Code Pen front and center on your website to allow developers to try it out and reduce friction for people considering using the product
- **Action (marketing/product experience):** Put the

documentation links front and center on the home page,
understanding how key they are to the decision process

2. New website headline

- "I guess I was curious as to whether or not it actually made
  it that simple."
- "And based on [the documentation], I was like, if it's really
  this easy, then I don't see why I wouldn't use it."
- "I think I had it working in five minutes."
- "So I just kind of got my account set up, dropped in the
  React component, and there, it really just worked."
- **Action (marketing):** Write a headline to the effect of "Up
  and running in five minutes. It really is as easy as it looks."
  and put it on our homepage/landing page

3. Testimonials

- "I think I had it working in five minutes...Oh, man, I was
  elated. So I just kind of got my account set up, dropped in
  the React component, and there, it really just worked. It's up
  and working. And it's beautiful."
- **Action (marketing):** Email him asking if you can use a
  quote from him as a testimonial
- **Action (marketing):** See if other current users would be
  willing to give testimonials
- **Action (marketing):** Put those testimonials on the site,
  ideally with them attesting to how "quick and on with your
  work" the product is

4. New landing pages

- Question to consider: How can you reach people when
  they're at that point of struggle? Perhaps some landing

pages targeting common specific integration issues people might have with competitors?

- "I don't want to say [I was] unsure of how the Amazon S3[2] buckets and stuff worked. I knew that's what it connected to and that's how it worked. But I've heard a bunch of people get frustrated about how complicated that would be."
- "I was so white knuckling to holding on to our current solution that the thought hadn't even registered."
- The point of switching is a point of frustration and landing pages should recognize the work users have already put in: "We just kept hitting brick walls with the storage...I was at my wits' end."
- **Action (competitor research):** Do some experimentation to see how competitor integrations might break, and do some research on Reddit/HackerNews/StackOverflow/their support forums to find some common snags
- **Action (marketing):** Write landing pages about common integration issues with competitors
- **Action (feature):** Compatibility mode for people switching from competitors?

LONGER-TERM THOUGHTS

1. Role of social proof during struggle

- "Oh, no, it never occurred to me [to try something else]. I was gonna continue banging my head on the keyboard. But a friend in the virtual coffee community said, 'Hey, why don't you just try this thing?'"
- "I heard about it through two different ways. I heard about it in a virtual coffee community I'm in. And then I also heard about it through the Twitterverse."
- **Strategy consideration:** Building brand awareness will be

important. People may not be looking for an alternative. How might you build brand awareness through the pricing model or marketing? After the company gains more free cash flow, worth considering community or conference sponsorships?

2. Competitor comparison landing pages

- Competitor pricing models create uncertainty and mental overhead: "The other options that I knew were out there usually had [an] up-front paywall that—well, I guess not up-front paywall, it was kind of a pay-as-you-go, depending on what you use. And I didn't know what those numbers would equate to. So where we were in the project, I didn't want to invest too much mental overhead into trying to figure that out. I really wanted to stay focused on just building the thing."
- **Insight:** A clear pricing model reduces potential customers' nervousness about using the product
- **Action (marketing):** Competitor comparison landing pages showing differences in pricing and features.

3. Product category is sticky

- "I was so white knuckling to holding on to our current solution that the thought hadn't even registered."
- Learned that while integrating file upload is a one-time process, people are hesitant to switch once they have it working (Sticky! This is probably why competitors can have convoluted pricing that people pay without understanding why they're being charged), and that the need for file uploads is frequent.
- **Insight:** The pain of switching combined with frequent need for the product is a very strong indicator for the long-term viability of this business
- **Action (product experience):** How many users are

activating after sign-up? When are they activating? Do we
have any indications about how soon someone might need
to activate in order to stay around as a customer? What can
we try to increase activation—documentation, onboarding
calls, etc?

[PART 10]
WHAT NOW?

If you've gotten this far, it shows how much you care about creating valuable products and services for real people.

It shows that you recognize that other peoples' perspectives are worth understanding.

It shows that you're willing to put in the work.

It shows that you're willing to suspend your own ideas and assumptions and perhaps even delight in your initial ideas and assumptions being incomplete.

It shows that you're willing to listen—really, deeply *listen*—to people in a way that may have been previously unfamiliar to you.

It shows that when you are confronted with a decision and find yourself saying, "I think people will want to...", you'll be able to catch yourself and remember that asking people is an option and that you have the tools to make it lead to useful results.

I hope you remember that this book is here to act as a springboard and is your toolbox for getting useful information from customers and potential customers.

I hope you carry through the empathy you've deployed in your interviews to your business decisions and interactions with others.

I hope it helps you consider how and what you would want to happen if you were the customer yourself.

I also hope you'll let me know what you got out of this book and will share this book with others if you learned something from it.

You can email me at michele@deployempathy.com, even if it's just to say hi and tell me what this book made you think about.

I also find it incredibly delightful when people tweet out a picture of their copy of the book. Please tag me @mjwhansen or the book's account, @DeployEmpathy.

[53]

RELATED TOPICS

My goal with this book was to only write about things that aren't covered in depth in other books.

Accordingly, there are a lot of important topics that are intentionally excluded.

This is not a comprehensive guide on starting a business, a comprehensive guide to user research, an in-depth exploration of processing or disseminating results, focused on physical products, or focused on accessibility.

This section aims to be a springboard for those other topics. These resources range from books to courses.

STARTING A BUSINESS

If you are trying to start a company and are reading this book to help, I have a tremendous amount of respect for you. Listening to customers is a free resource that so many companies overlook, so you are putting yourself ahead by putting your potential customers first.

However, this is not a comprehensive guide to starting a business. Thankfully, many books on that topic already exist.

If you like courses, Amy Hoy and Alex Hillman's *30x500* is the gold standard of courses on starting a small internet business, and their book *Just Fucking Ship* is worth reading if you prefer books.

If you're getting started on your own without venture funding and prefer a book, I suggest Arvid Kahl's *Zero to Sold*.

MORE RIGOROUS CUSTOMER RESEARCH

There's a line in veteran user researcher Steve Portigal's book *Interviewing Users* that jumped at me when I first read it: "Much of this presumes that the fieldwork team is assembled from two types of people: those who are likely to be reading this book, and those who wouldn't even have imagined a book like this existed."

This book is written with that latter group in mind.

If you're a user researcher or designer, you probably already know most of the content in this book. You may notice that I imply but skip over a lot of the philosophy of Jobs To Be Done and activity theory. This is not a comprehensive guide, and that is on purpose, as I am attempting to only write about tactics that are not covered in depth in other books.

Instead, I hope this book can serve as a book that you can recommend to others as an accessible introduction to talking to customers.

My personal favorite books on user research written at a more rigorous level are Steve Portigal's *Interviewing Users*, Jim Kalbach's *Jobs to Be Done Playbook*, and Indi Young's *Mental Models*.

PROCESSING AND DISSEMINATING RESULTS

This book is not an in-depth exploration of the different ways of processing and sharing results. I intentionally don't go deep on job maps, journey mapping, or getting institutional buy-in to research results. I'm writing with smaller companies and teams in mind, and in my experience, there tends to be fewer formal processes in those companies.

I suggest Jim Kalbach's *The Jobs to Be Done Playbook* as a companion to this book if you are looking for an accessible overview of the different analysis methods. *The User's Journey* by Donna Lichaw and *Service Design* by Andy Polaine, Ben Reason & Lavrans Løvlie are also wonderful resources.

QUANTITATIVE RESEARCH

This book doesn't go into the quantitative side of user research, which is a worthy and necessary effort. I believe that quantitative and qualitative research are not an either/or and instead should be used together as part of a broader effort to understand customers. I do this as part of my own decision-making process, and there are a lot of books on it. If you want a book on survey methodologies, designing A/B tests, or analytics, this is not that book.

You might look to *Quantifying the User Experience: Practical Statistics for User Research* by Jeff Sauro and James R. Lewis. Erika Hall's *Just Enough Research* also discusses other research methods.

USABILITY OR ACCESSIBILITY

I mention usability in the context of screen share interviews, but this is not a book on usability or accessibility.

Usability testing can help you uncover which parts of a product or prototype are difficult to use, and it's a tool that should be in your toolbox.

I encourage you to incorporate people who might need accommodations to use your product into your research, whether those accommodations be required for mental, physical, or linguistic/cultural reasons. Accessibility is worth designing for and devoting attention to, and encompasses everything from accommodating slow internet connections to disabilities and more. Leaving out people with disabilities means leaving out people, and that can mean missing out on opportunities.

Accessibility should be part of your design and engineering decision-making.

For more, see *Accessibility for Everyone* by Lara Kalbag.

[54]
FURTHER READING

The shelf near my desk was full of books as I wrote this book. I've mentioned the most significant ones to the development of this book here, as well as a few other resources you may find helpful.

How To Talk So Kids Will Listen and Listen So Kids Will Talk

If you find the techniques in "How to Talk So People Will Talk" are wholly unfamiliar, it might be worth your time to read this book—even if you aren't a parent. It can be difficult to listen actively when we haven't been shown it ourselves.

Much of good UX practice is also good human being practice, and this book is a practical guide for good human being practice. I've also taken inspiration from it in structuring this book.

Nonviolent Communication is also an excellent primer on empathetic communication in a wide variety of situations, from international politics to the workplace to marriage.

Never Split the Difference

When I was in business school, I took a one-semester course on negotiations. The skills I learned in that one class alone more than paid for the entire cost of the degree within a year of me taking that class. But not everyone can attend an in-person negotiations class for three months. This book is the next best thing.

Even if you aren't in sales, you'll find this book useful. Many of the techniques for negotiations are shared in customer interviewing. The difference is that negotiations have a motivated outcome of the conversation, whereas an interview does not.

Practical Empathy

Indi Young is a master of the application of empathy to business. This is one of my most recommended books.

The Jobs to Be Done Playbook

This book is heavily indebted to the Jobs to Be Done framework but is purposefully light on theory to be as actionable as possible.

Jim Kalbach does a great job providing a concise, clear, actionable overview of the Jobs to Be Done framework. He is balanced and detailed while keeping it moving and actionable.

The second half of this book is particularly good for those who are in 20-plus person companies where more structured methods of documentation and insight sharing are helpful.

Interviewing Users

Steve Portigal is a master of interviewing. While this book is written with user research consultants in mind (think: physically traveling to customers, larger budgets), there are tons of practical lessons about how to conduct oneself in an interview. His *Doorbells, Danger, and Dead Batteries* is an entertaining romp through interviewers' war stories.

What Got You Here Won't Get You There

If you've been socialized to feel the need to prove yourself and your potential, this book might be helpful for you. It certainly was for me. So many of the conversational habits that must be suppressed when interviewing—interrupting, offering one's own ideas, correcting people—come out of educational and work environments where we are constantly competing with others and have to prove ourselves. This book is a gentle and honest invitation to reflect on where those behaviors might come from and how you can overcome them.

Sales Safari [course]

If you want to start an online business but don't know where to start, this is the course to take. Amy Hoy and Alex Hillman walk you through how to decide on an audience, how to find them, and how to figure out what their pain points are by observing them.

The User Experience Team of One

If you are within a small-but-not-tiny team (3-30 people) and the only one doing UX work as part of your role, this book belongs on your shelf. It scales down key UX research concepts and processes like customer discovery, journey mapping, and service design for a one-person UX team.

Badass: Making Users Awesome

If I had to pick only one book to introduce people to thinking about products from a user's perspective, this book would be it. If I were giving a gift to a new graduate who intended to work in tech, I would give them this book along with *Never Split The Difference*.

The Mom Test

This book is one of the most popular primers on why you shouldn't ask people whether they think a business is a good idea or whether they would buy something. Many of the early readers of this book said *The Mom Test* was a lightbulb moment for them when they realized not to ask those questions, and set them off on a journey to find more effective ways to talk to customers.

APPENDIX A: CHEAT SHEET

If there's something specific you're eager to solve, this section will help you skip around based on specific problems.

No matter the challenge, you will need to use the conversation principles in Part VI, "How to Talk So People Will Talk." You will also need to prepare for interviews (Chapter 38).

YOU HAVE AN IDEA AND WANT TO EVALUATE IT

- **Process:** Chapter 17 (Research loops)
- **Recruiting users:** Chapters 19 (Reddit), 20 (Twitter), and/or 21 (LinkedIn)
- **Script:** Chapter 39 (Discovery Script) and *optionally* Chapter 44 (Card Sorting) then Chapter 43 (interactive interviews for prototype testing)
- **Viability**: Chapter 9 (Viable, usable, valuable, feasible), Chapter 46 (How to ask people what they would pay for something)

- **Analysis**: Chapter 49 (Pain and Frequency Matrix) and Chapter 48 (Drawing a simple customer journey map)
- *Note: it may also make sense to do Switch interviews on people who've recently started using a competitor product*

YOU HAVE SOMETHING LAUNCHED, AND WANT TO FIGURE OUT WHY PEOPLE AREN'T BUYING/WHY THEY'RE DROPPING OFF/ETC.

- **Recruiting users:** Chapter 19 (Reddit) if you don't have any users, Chapter 23 (Email) if you do, even if they aren't paying
- **Script:** Chapter 44 (interactive interviews) or Chapter 41 (Switch interview) if people have bought

YOU WANT TO GET MORE CUSTOMERS

- **Process:** Chapter 18 (Ongoing research)
- **Recruiting users:** Chapter 23 (Email) and Chapter 24 (Surveys)
- **Scripts:** Chapter 40 (Switch interview) and Chapter 41 (long-time customer interview)

YOU WANT TO KNOW WHY PEOPLE CANCEL

- **Process:** Chapter 18 (Ongoing research)
- **Recruiting users:** Chapter 23 (Email) and Chapter 24 (Surveys)
- **Scripts:** Chapter 42 (Cancellation interview) and Chapter 41 (long-time customer interview)

YOU WANT TO FIGURE OUT WHAT YOU SHOULD BUILD NEXT FOR AN
EXISTING PRODUCT

- **Process:** Chapter 15 (project-based research) and Chapter
  16 (How many people should you interview?)
- **Recruiting users:** Chapter 23 (Email) and Chapter 24
  (Surveys)
- **Scripts:** Chapter 40 (Switch interview) and Chapter 41
  (long-time customer interview)
- **Analysis**: Chapter 48 (Drawing a simple customer journey
  map)

YOU WANT PEOPLE TO STOP COMPLAINING ABOUT A SPECIFIC FEATURE
OR WONDER WHY THEY KEEP REQUESTING SOMETHING

- **Process**: Chapter 56 (Appendix B), Feature requests as
  customer research
- **Scripts**: Chapter 41 (long-time customers) and/or Chapter
  43 (interactive interviews)

APPENDIX B: FOR FOUNDERS

This part speaks to the specific situations that founders and would-be founders of small software companies might find themselves in, including:

- Finding time for research as a solo founder
- Turning feature requests into customer support
- The differences and overlap between sales, customer support, and customer research
- Troubleshooting common difficult customer support situations empathetically (including templates)
- A vignette from my own company, Geocodio, on how we use research as part of our overall goal-setting

[55]

RESEARCH AS A SOLO FOUNDER

A developer friend of mine with several successful side projects read an early draft of this book, and they said something that stuck with me:

""I honestly hadn't really thought about doing customer interviews post launch... especially in the self-funded software world, all the writing on customer development talks about doing it prior to launch (or product market fit)."

I realized that they were right: in the world of small software companies, people will talk about the importance of talking to customers prior to building, prior to launching, or while getting post-launch feedback. But there is less discussion about already up-and-running businesses listening to customers as a way to grow even more.

Surely people are getting feedback from their customers all the time. Feature requests. Bugs. Issues.

Yet you're missing out on so much if you aren't taking the time to sit down and ask people—new and existing customers alike—why they need what you do in the first place.

That's my view, at least.

For my company, Geocodio, customer feedback is how we figure out what to work on. What to fix, what to tweak, what to add, what to think about overhauling entirely. It is the lifeblood of our company.

We do project-based research when we have specific questions, and we do ongoing research as part of our everyday workflow.

Customer research should be integrated into your existing workflow, rather than being something that makes you feel like you need to drop everything, stop building, go research for a while, and then come back.

You will find your own rhythm.

[56]

FEATURE REQUESTS AS CUSTOMER RESEARCH

It makes sense if the idea of customer research sounds like more work on top of what you're already doing… maybe more work than you can take on.

So let's talk about a situation you're probably in frequently that is an easy springboard to deploying customer research skills.

It usually starts something like this:

"Hey, have you all ever considered adding…"

or

"I was just wondering if you could make it so I could…"

or

"Can you add the ability to…"

Otherwise known as: feature requests.

Which, let's face it, sometimes align with what you're already planning to do, but often don't. People are trying to be helpful…yet when you feel like you've already got more than enough to do and not nearly enough time, they may not be the most delightful thing to receive. It might feel like more work. Work that hasn't been fully scoped out, thought through, and prioritized against existing work.

But what if you could use those feature requests as a springboard to learn more about the customers' overall needs?

The purpose of this isn't to convince you to be open to every feature request and change your roadmap every time you get one.

Far from it.

I want to open you to the idea that feature requests can be a welcome and crisp window into an acute problem for a customer. They're aware they have a problem, though they are articulating it as a solution rather than a problem. You can then use customer research skills to dig into where that request is coming from and why it would help their process, which you can then use to build out your own understanding of what they're trying to do.

My point here is to take feature requests from something that might be met with a groan into something that inspires curiosity and leaves you understanding your customers better. That maybe, even a little, leaves you excited about learning something new and more motivated—even if you don't build what they asked or in the exact way they asked for it.

That's why it's important that you pause your brains from jumping to whether a specific feature would be possible or how you might implement it or issues with how the customer (or leader or coworker, if you're in a larger company) has presented the solution.

With a feature request, try to dig into the context of why someone needs something and when they would use it. If you can, you also want to dig into who is requesting it. (If it's a higher-up who has final say over buying your software, you want to know that information.) You probably instinctually jump to thinking through whether it's possible and how you might implement it, but I have to ask you to tamp down that urge until you've figured out what the person is truly asking for.

FEATURE REQUEST RESPONSE TEMPLATE: PHONE

If you happen to receive one on the phone—say, on a support call or sales call, or in an interview, here are some questions you can use:

- *Can you walk me through the context on when you might use this?*
- *How did this project come about?*
- *What do you currently use for this/What did you use for this in the past?*
- *Do you pay anything for those [other tools]? Is there anything else those [other tools] are used for?*
- *Can you walk me through what you've already considered?*
- *Can you walk me through the different steps of the project?*
- *Can you show me what you do now? (ask for screen share)*
- *How much time does this currently take you?*
- *Is there anyone else on your end involved?*

You can hear an example of responding to a feature request here around the nineteen minute mark in the example interview:

Michele: Well, thank you so much for taking the time to talk to me. I've learned so much from you. Is there anything else you think I should know?

Drew: I guess now that we've been talking about it, I do have a question—and this would probably end up being a feature request more than anything. But are there plans in the future to, from the Simple File Upload dashboard, to be able to section off different stuff? You know, maybe this is type A files versus type B? Or is that already there and I haven't seen it?

Michele: So I can't speak to that, because I don't work on it myself, but could you walk me through how that would fit into your process, or how that would help you?

Drew: Sure. We're going to be rolling out some user accounts. There's gonna be two different types of accounts...

By the way, for those of you in larger companies, these questions will work just as well with internal customers who bring feature requests. Just remember to ask them in your most harmless voice possible, lest it come off like you're challenging them. (I learned that one the hard way.)

FEATURE REQUEST RESPONSE TEMPLATE: TEXT

If someone emails (or Slacks, or posts on Twitter, etc.) you a feature suggestion, first try to get them to elaborate. The goal is to get back a three- or four-paragraph response with their full process, and which you can then ask more follow-up questions about. Most of the time, I can pull that out with one of the following responses.

Your reply should be short and open ended.

I encourage you not to ask more than two questions in these emails, otherwise the response rate tends to plummet. (Though it may be tempting, your goal is not to ask so many questions that people give up.)

The formula is: 1) thank them, 2) ask for broader context, 3) use a deferential tense (could, would, might), and 4) use positive clarification words (curious, wondering)

Try to use words that elicit explanation about the broader situation, like:

- context
- background
- broader goal/process
- big picture

Thank you for this suggestion! Could you walk me through a bit about when you would need this and what it would help you do overall? I'm interested to know how you currently solve this, even if it's manual or uses other tools.

Thank you for taking the time to share this idea! I'm curious—might you be able to give me the broader context on how this would fit into your overall process? I'm interested to hear how you currently solve this.

Thanks for suggesting this! Would you be able to tell me a little bit more about what you're trying to do overall and how this would fit in? I'm wondering if you might be able to walk me through a specific situation where this would help you.

CATALOGUING FEATURE REQUESTS

There's a lot you can do with these learnings. I'm going to touch on two here that we do at Geocodio, and you can use them as a springboard for how you handle these requests yourself.

When we've gotten a response from someone, I always like to thank them for sharing the suggestion. They took the time to send a message about this, so clearly it's important to them and they thought it was a good idea. That deserves acknowledgement, even if it isn't something that fits onto a roadmap or company vision.

The one thing you should always do is add whatever you have learned to your bank of customer understanding. We might make those deposits formally into some sort of system, for example:

- Attach notes to the customer's account (CRM, customer support platform, etc)
- Email notes to yourself
- Save them into a spreadsheet or other tool for capturing feedback

The second only applies if it is something that is directionally aligned, even if not immediate. I always save the idea and tag the customer, and keep a running list of ideas with each customer that requested it. I tell customers we're saving their idea and will reach out if/when we add it. (The "if" is key there.) We use GitHub issues for saving suggestions because it's already integrated into Intercom, and it works for us. There are a variety of other tools you can use for this, whether it's a spreadsheet or a tool designed specifically for categorizing feedback.

If we have a bunch of customers speaking to the same process and general idea for a long time, we'll try to make those features happen. Those saved lists are helpful for reaching back out for more context or people who can help us refine/scope a feature and test it if we decide to move forward.

At a minimum, if we do add a requested feature, we then reach back out to everyone who requested it or mentioned a related use case. Sometimes that means emailing someone who made a feature request a month, six months, two years, even five years ago. I used to feel a bit worried about emailing people with such a long delay, but I've found that people are utterly delighted that we remembered and made it happen, even if it's years later. I have been floored with how appreciative people have been.

I like to think it's moments like that when you seal the trust you build by listening to your customers: you listen in the moment when the pain is acute, and you show that you listened by returning to them months or years later.

We might be businesspeople, but the operative word there is *people*. All people like to feel valued, appreciated, and helpful. And being appreciative and curious when someone comes to you with a request is just a small way you can go beyond being another faceless business and to an empathetic one that truly cares about the people it serves.

[57]

SALES, CUSTOMER SUPPORT, AND CUSTOMER RESEARCH

Most of this book is presented as a jumping-off point. It is intentionally somewhat loose.

This chapter, by contrast, is going to be more prescriptive. It is vitally important that you mentally separate sales, customer support, and customer research, and act differently in those settings.

Customer research is a specific activity to unearth customers' underlying goals, activities, frustrations, and needs, and we use those insights across the many different functions of the business. These things can trickle out in sales and customer support, but I encourage you to set aside time to get these sorts of insights in a concentrated form.

I hope you'll forgive my pedantry on this. I just want to save you from an accidentally awkward situation. I feel confident you can avoid that once you have a sense for where the lines are.

Let's dive in a bit, starting with customer support.

CUSTOMER SUPPORT IS NOT CUSTOMER RESEARCH

When someone approaches customer support, it's usually because there is a problem. Something is broken, doesn't make sense, and is getting in their way. And chances are, they'd rather do the thing than talk to someone about how they can't do the thing.

After all, no one *wants* to be standing in the return line at H&M.

(I say this knowing that every organization has its "frequent flyers": people who tend to call and talk quite a bit because they have limited people to talk to in their daily lives in a consumer-facing business, or have frequent bug reports in business-facing business. In my experience answering phones, those people are only a small percentage of customer support inquiries, but garner an outsize amount of attention.)

So, someone comes to you for support. They are approaching you because there is a problem, and this problem stands in the way of accomplishing their task, and they need this problem fixed so they can get on with whatever it was they were trying to do in the first place. You use empathy here to understand their frustration, and help them resolve it and get back to whatever it was they were doing before they hit this snag.

But the kind of deep curiosity about their underlying tasks is not appropriate in this scenario. They're trying to get something done, and the product is already in their way, so it isn't appropriate to get in their way further with more questions.

Note, you can use this as an opportunity to follow up later—once the problem is solved, the task is done, and the stress of accomplishing the task has evaporated—to set up a dedicated interview another day. This might look like sending them an email a week later like this:

Hi [Person],

I just wanted to thank you for your understanding last week as we worked through [issue]. Thank you for surfacing this. By speaking up, you've allowed us to fix this and ensure that no one else encounters that frustration again.

When we were talking, you briefly mentioned how you were trying to [broader activity that relates to underlying goal]. I was wondering if we might find time sometime this week or next to talk about how you [accomplish underlying goal] to help us understand what you do better.

[Scheduling information—ex, calendar link]

Thanks,

You

And on that note, customer interviews are not customer support. If someone surfaces an issue or complaint, you should jot it down, tell them you're taking note of it and will communicate it to the appropriate person/team/get it in the bug queue afterward, and then dive into why that problem presented a problem for the customer. This can be a great launching point into descriptions of processes, but you should not go into customer support mode.

SALES IS NOT CUSTOMER RESEARCH

Sales is not customer research as well, but for an entirely different reason. On sales calls, it's common to get into the problems that someone is solving, the tools they've used before or are evaluating, and why they might be looking to switch.

This is great information, but it's incomplete information.

To fully understand someone's goals, activities, and needs, you need to be able to dig into the emotion and social context behind the tasks. You need to deeply understand the struggle and pain from the person's perspective.

But in a sales situation, people have their guard up. For good reason! That should be respected.

Sales is usually a low-trust setting: someone is trying to figure out whether your product is a fit. It's a trust-building opportunity for sure, but it's not by nature a relaxed setting, and it is therefore not appropriate to dive to the emotional level that you would in an interview.

In a sales setting, you might also give advice. If a person voices a problem they need solved that your product doesn't do, you might say that we're planning to add that in the future and ask why they need it, or that another competitor solves it better and recommend they use them instead. Because it shows your own judgment and perspective, it would not be appropriate to provide advice or information like that in an interview.

On the flip side, customer interviews are not sales.

This is probably the biggest mistake I see people making with customer research.

If someone surfaces a problem that they need solved that another product of ours solves and they don't realize it, do not tell them.

I recognize this may have you scratching your head, and perhaps frustrate you a bit. But this is an important urge to check because nothing pops the bubble of trust faster than trying to sell someone.

Whether it's an existing feature they already pay for, an add-on product, or a separate product entirely—don't sell them. These are signs that discoverability of that feature/product is low, and we can dive more into what context they might expect to have that problem solved, the tasks it's adjacent to, and so forth, so you can learn how to better position that product in terms of process flow.

(And you can always email them later. There's a template for this in Chapter 38, "Interview Preparation.")

IN CONCLUSION

You use empathy in customer support, but it isn't appropriate to use too much curiosity and pepper them with questions. They encountered a problem and just want to get on with what they were trying to do. Don't get in their way any more than the product issue already has.

You use curiosity in sales. But it isn't appropriate to plunge their emotional depths and use the kind of empathy you would in an interview. You shouldn't force them to take down the emotional guardrails they have justifiably put up in such a low-trust setting.

You use empathy and curiosity in customer research. When you intentionally interview a person, you dive into their goals, their pain, their process, their emotions.

Customer support, sales, and customer research should work together, and can do so beautifully. But you need to regard them as their own distinct activities, with different ways you conduct them, in order to get the results you want.

[58]

CUSTOMER SUPPORT

Note: This chapter is written for founders of small companies. If that doesn't apply to you, feel free to skip this.

I'm going to speak directly to the founders for a moment.

You're probably *talking* to customers a lot. But how much are you *listening* to them?

Founders of small software companies, especially during the side-project and early full-time periods, talk to customers a lot. It's pretty common for people to handle all customer support and sales themselves for a long time. (We still do and have no plans to change!). Lots of phone calls, emails, chats with customers.

So I am under no illusion about the majority of your customer interactions.

Someone having an issue. Someone saying your site doesn't work (when the problem is that they're using Internet Explorer.) People asking to reset their passwords. People asking you to add a new feature.

By contrast, customer research seems like a calm oasis. A faraway tropical beach where you can luxuriate in proactive product development.

Customer support? Reactive. Unpredictable. Sometimes quite stressful.

...especially when people are upset.

And so given that the majority of your customer interactions as a very, very small software company owner will be in the customer support context, it feels worth diving into here.

Empathy is an incredibly powerful tool for product development and figuring out what to build. It's also a powerful tool for defusing customer support situations and turning them into opportunities to learn more about the customer's use case and overall goals.

I will not claim that it is easy. Providing empathetic customer support is a skill – one that way too many companies undervalue.

It's especially hard when the customer is genuinely wrong. The customer is not always right, but they are always right about *their experience*.[1] The customer's underlying feeling has to be validated, even if they themselves did something that contributed to the situation. (If they did do something that led to the issue, you can phrase in the passive voice, absolving them of responsibility.)

It's hard.

Yet I know you can learn it. (Even people who are conflict averse.)

In keeping with the practical toolkit approach of this book, I'm going to provide a few sample response templates below.

But before we do that, I want to tell you a story.

THE GRUMBLING USERS

Nate Bosscher is a software development consultant who was working with a client to build a new system that would be used by multiple departments. The project had been going great for several months, and toward the end, it came time to onboard another department that would be using the software.

On the onboarding call, people from this department were clearly unhappy. They were finding every chance they could to snipe at the product and grumble about having to use it.

Before I continue, I want you to notice what your instinctive reaction would be to this situation. (Not the one that you think you should have after reading this book... but what the first one that comes to mind is.)

Is it to ignore them? Is it to silently roll your eyes and try to get the call over with? Is it to call them out for their boorish behavior?

Nate took a different approach.

He was able to short-circuit that "Gahh, people complaining" response. The people in this department were critical to the entire company's successful adoption of the software, so he found time to listen to them on their own in a separate venue. (This is Right Thing to Do #1)

When he got them on the phone, he didn't call them out, or prepare a defense about the software, or have his client explain the value of the software. He instead let them rant... for half an hour. (This is Right Thing to Do #2)

This is powerful because it makes people feel heard. They didn't feel heard by the software, and that led to their grumbling on the call.

One thing about learning how to show empathy is that you might start seeing how many people were never shown empathy themselves growing up, and consequently really need to receive some as adults in order to process their own feelings.

Even the adult men Nate was dealing with.

They just needed to feel heard.

Nate realized that, and that allowed him to defuse his own feelings of rejection (*They didn't like what he'd built!*) to center their unprocessed feelings (They didn't feel *included* —the software and whoever built it was beside the point.)

After they were able to process their feelings, Nate was able to get to the root of the issue: it turned out that the software didn't quite match some paper forms they were used to. The mental model was off.

The solution?

Rearranging some form fields.

He made the changes, sent it back to them, and they were thrilled. The software now matched their familiar physical model, and they were ready to go.

Now, the solution isn't always so simple. Yet the thread to pull from this is to validate people first—even if they're acting in a way that isn't exactly constructive. Validate the person first and the problem they're experiencing.

Without further ado... let's stock up your toolbox for those customer support interactions, shall we?

TEMPLATE: YOU MESSED SOMETHING UP, AND SOMEONE IS UNHAPPY

Okay, this is harder, so we're doing this second.

(But it's also critical. And so easy to get wrong.)

Think back to the worst customer support experience you've ever had.

Got it in your head?

Ok.

I'm willing to bet there was some combination of the following:

- The person you were talking to was not empowered to solve your problem.
- They told you the problem you had didn't exist.
- They told you that the way you were using [their thing] was wrong.
- They told you what you wanted to do overall was wrong.
- They were straight-up unreachable or unavailable for support.
- They did something shady, like not refunding you when you had a valid reason.

Let me tell you a story about something that happened to me at my first job out of college.

The company had an online fundraising product, and the name of the product would show on people's credit card statements. (This was in pre-Stripe days.) So fairly often, we'd get people calling our small office asking "What the heck is this charge from [product] on my credit card?" and we'd have to look up the charges manually and tell them whom they had donated to.

As the lowliest member of the office, I was the one who answered the phone. I'd worked in retail and various other settings where I'd had to talk to customers, so I felt fairly adept at this. People would ask where the charge was from with a hint of annoyance, and I'd explain it was a fundraising product and ask if they'd made any donations lately. Usually that would connect the dots, but if not, I would transfer them to my coworker who had access to the database of donations, and they'd be on their way.

This happened several times per day.

One day, a woman called in. The tone in her voice suggested she thought it was a scam.

I explained to her that it was a fundraising product and perhaps she'd made a donation recently, and that perhaps she could search her email for the amount and find the receipt.

Growing more agitated, she demanded I tell her what she'd donated to.

Except I didn't have access to the database, so I couldn't... and my coworker who handled those requests was at a two-hour meeting with a client.

I told her I could take her information and we'd get back to her later in the day when he was back.

She continued demanding that I tell her and accused us of running a scam. And I kept calmly telling her that I didn't have access to the information and we'd get back to her.

"So what are you then, just a fixture?" she spat at me, exasperated.

I momentarily considered my own similarities with the lamp sitting on my desk, feeling a kinship that had never occurred to me before.

I can't tell you how that conversation ended, but I can tell you I never forgot it.

Thinking back to it now, I notice that I used language that I thought would placate her ("I understand you're upset"). I probably tried to interrupt as her language and tone escalated. But I did not use any of the skills I now know:

- Apologizing (!) Apologies are powerful and effective ways of defusing a situation. I was following the old school advice to never apologize, and that was a mistake. I should have said, "I'm sorry I can't fix this for you. This is frustrating, and you deserve to be able to get to the bottom of this quickly and get on with your day.")
- Mirroring ("Your credit card was charged, and you can't think of a non-profit you donated to recently.")
- Using listening words ("Mhm")
- Labeling her emotion ("It makes sense you're upset I don't have access to the database, and you don't believe me that I don't have access.")

People are often afraid to say that a customer is annoyed, upset, or frustrated to them directly, because they're afraid it will remind the person how upset they are.

As Chris Voss explains in *Never Split the Difference*, labeling emotions in particular does the opposite: it helps defuse them. As Voss says, "The fastest and most efficient means of establishing a quick working relationship is to acknowledge the negative." By hearing someone else describe themselves as upset, they feel heard, and it allows the conversation to start to calm down.

So.

The idea here?

Validate them as a person and the problem they're having first. Without getting defensive. Without explaining to them what was supposed to happen, or what they are doing wrong. See them first.

And if you're in a position of leadership, empower people doing customer support to truly solve the customer's problem.

Phrasing

Phrasing is really important here, and what you need to make sure to avoid is fake empathy—the kind you so often see in public apologies. It might feel to you like you're showing concern yet these phrases just make things worse by creating distance between how you, the speaker, feels, and how the other person feels. Don't use them! (This goes for personal life too.)

- I'm sorry you feel that way.
- I'm sorry you see it that way.
- I'm sorry you were confused by that.
- I'm sorry that wasn't clear to you.

These phrases often come up as expressions of sympathy, which Brené Brown's research has shown creates distance and further anguish on the part of the person expressing the problem. "I'm sorry you feel that way" is dismissive, while "This is frustrating" is validating. ("This is frustrating for you" is dismissive and isolating, since it implies that they are the only one who would feel that way and that their frustration with the situation is not shared.)

Better phrases center their problem, center the other person, and validate their experience, like:

- This is causing a problem for you.
- It seems like this could work better for what you're trying to do.
- It sounds like you expected this to work a different way.
- That should not have happened, and it makes sense you're frustrated.

Notice that those phrases center the person rather than the speaker ("I can understand why're you're frustrated" versus "It makes sense you're frustrated.") By using passive construction ("This is a problem"), their frustration also sounds more like a fact rather than a nebulous feeling, which is reassuring and calming.

People are also sometimes afraid to apologize, as if doing so means that everything the other person has done is right. An introductory "I apologize. It sounds like..." can work wonders. Don't be afraid to apologize.

YOU'VE MESSED SOMETHING UP, AND THEY'RE UPSET

Let's say you have an outage. Someone is pretty justified in being mad in that scenario.

The best thing you can do is be proactive and notify them of the outage before they are even aware of it. This way, they know you're on it.

The points you want to hit are:

- What happened
- You recognize their situation [i.e., affirm their feeling]
- You're aware of the issue
- [You've fixed it]
- [You've credited their account for the downtime, if applicable]
- You're doing things to prevent it from ever happening again

Sometimes people come to you, and you have to find a way to respond that acknowledges the problem and centers their experience.

For example:

Customer: Uhh, is your API down? Our app is 404ing because of this! This is a serious problem.

You: Yes, our API is down. We are actively working to fix this problem and will update you as soon as it is fixed. We will write an after-action report that details what happened and what we are doing to prevent it from happening again.

Everyone fucks things up.

But not everyone follows up or does the work necessary to make sure it never happens again.

For the developers reading who want to start their own businesses: the freedom to prioritize infrastructure work rather than doing a quick fix and getting back on the feature release treadmill is one of the great perks of having your own company. If you're tired of being paged on the weekends to hot fix someone else's code and know your PM will never let you prioritize paying down tech debt, know that there is a better world out there.

SOMEONE THINKS YOU DID SOMETHING WRONG, BUT YOU HAVEN'T

A customer accusing you of doing something wrong when you (or your product) haven't is an especially frustrating situation.

Let's say you get this one-line message from a customer:

Customer: You charged me a hundred dollars when it was supposed to be free!

Your first instinct may be to see if there's a problem with the billing code, only to then become annoyed when you've looked in every nook and cranny and everything seems to be fine.

At this point, you may be starting to simmer in your own correctness, and it is worth recognizing and naming that feeling ("I'm frustrated because they're accusing me of doing something wrong when I haven't").

This situation can bring up our earliest experiences of being unfairly accused on the playground, and it's worth allowing yourself to work through that for a moment before replying.

You: Would you be able to give me more context on how things happened from your perspective?

Customer: Well, I set this script up as a test, and then I guess I didn't realize it kept going, and you guys shouldn't have charged me for that, it should have known it was repeating...

Notice there are two parallel tracks there:

1. The person made a mistake (a script kept running without them realizing it)
2. Perhaps there's a usability improvement we could make on our end to make it clearer

If you're able to work through it with them to find the cause from their side, I encourage you to mirror it back to them in the passive voice, which simultaneously acknowledges the error was on their end and also absolves them of responsibility:

You: It sounds like a script ran when it wasn't supposed to. That's okay, mistakes happen. We will give you a one-time refund of [$]. We'll explore how we could alert customers when this might be happening. In the future, you can check your real-time balance at...

The template for this is thus:

- Acknowledge their mistake in the passive voice
- Refund/credit them (no matter the balance, someone who feels cheated is not worth the price)
- Acknowledge you could be more fault-tolerant on your end
- Tell them how they can avoid this in the future, independent of any changes on your end

Sometimes it's harder to dig for the context, and a person seems beyond the point of cooling down.

Let's dive into that.

SOMEONE IS INSULTING YOU

I urge you to try to distinguish between when someone is mad for a justifiable reason but comporting themselves appropriately (anger is a valid emotion and people are allowed to be mad) and when someone is being a bully.

Even if they have a good reason to be mad, there's no justification for toxic behavior.

Usually this stems from someone who only knows the fight response to difficult situations. They will usually exhaust themselves ranting, and eventually they will wait for a reaction from you.

I've only had this happen to me once in the thousands of calls I've had with customers, and it was a sales call.

Instead of reacting defensively, you can defuse them by relentlessly agreeing with them. They need to hear that they are right and feel validated before they can get to a calmer place. But not in the entirety —just with a small part of what they said.

This is a trick I learned in negotiations training, and it's helped me time after time.

For example:

Angry customer: Your software sucks! It doesn't do what I needed! How are you even in business! You are incompetent! I'm going to [threat]! [Tantrum!] [Rant!]

You: You're right, it sounds like our software didn't do what you needed. It makes sense you're frustrated. I'm going to go ahead and refund the charges now. I'm wondering if [competitor] might be a better fit for you. Would you like me to delete your account, or would you like to do so yourself at [link]?

Use phrases like "You're right" and "I can see what you mean" and "I agree." People who are in this mode need to hear that they are right before they can calm down. It doesn't even matter what you agree with, as long as they hear that.

But I want to be clear: just because the customer hears that they are right doesn't mean they're right. It doesn't mean you have to cater to them and put up with their toxicity.

So if you get in this scenario, the formula to follow is:

Tell them they're right, and then gently fire them.

Because who has time for people who treat us with disrespect?

I certainly don't.

(Let's go to a less upsetting example.)

SOMEONE REPORTS A BUG

The key here to show that you take them seriously is to reply as soon as possible and promise to follow up. There is a problem, they have to take time out of their day to tell you about it, and chances are there's someone else inside or outside their organization asking them about it. Your goal is to give them confidence that the issue will be resolved.

The key here is to acknowledge it as quickly as possible. You may be tempted to wait to reply until you can tell them it's fixed, but it's better to give them the comfort of knowing someone is looking at it first. (This seems to be an instinct that engineers in particular struggle with. I urge you to acknowledge the problem first, then fix it.)

It might go something like:

You: Thank you for bringing this to our attention. We will investigate this and get back to you [optional: include time frame].

I've found that, perhaps somewhat paradoxically, saying "We take this seriously" comes off as hollow, so the way you show that it's taken seriously is by replying quickly and following up in a timely manner.

The need for speed also applies to payment inquiries. The goal is to prevent it from becoming a chargeback. You first need to establish that you a) acknowledge them, b) are capable of helping them, and c) give them concrete places to figure out why they used your service.

Person: Why was I charged [$]? I don't even know what this is??

You: Hi, I can help you sort this out. It looks like you [did action on the product] on [date]. You can see that activity [here].

With payments, proactive is always better than reactive. No one likes a surprise bill. So any time you have pricing/payment/payment frequency questions, I encourage you to think about how you could communicate that proactively through transactional emails, documentation on your website, information in receipts, and so forth.

THEY'RE HAVING AN INSTALLATION/INTEGRATION ISSUE

I call this sort of scenario neutral because while they're not exactly happy, they usually aren't mad either. They want to use your product, and they're just having trouble getting it to work.

What you want to do is establish that you are there to help them, and that you are competent to do so.

This has similarities with people reporting bugs and feature requests. You want to:

- Ask for clarification about what they're trying to do overall
- Figure out what they've already tried to do in terms of the installation

It might go something like….

Customer: Hi, I can't get your Python library to work.

You: I'm happy to help you with this. Can you share some more specifics on what you're trying to do and where things seem to be going wrong?

IT'S NOT ALL BAD

It might seem from this like customer support is not a very fun part of running a very small company. It's a skill to learn, and it makes sense why the first hire a lot of people make is customer support.

I found that once you get a handle on the basic concept of validating people first, and get over the fear of angry customers, it gets a lot easier. More often than not, it's an untapped well for ideas about how to improve a product.

And also… the vast majority of customer service interactions tend to be more neutral. People making a sales inquiry. Basic questions about the service or pricing.

Occasionally, truly amazing compliments. Just the other day, we got one from someone about how our service had directly positively impacted her career path within the company she works for.

So I hope this doesn't scare you.

I hope it gives you some confidence, or at the very least, something to fall back on in those harder situations.

If you only remember one thing from this, let it be:

Validate the person first.

RESEARCH FOR GOAL SETTING

Customer portfolio analysis is our primary way of goal setting at Geocodio.

Our top line goal is revenue stability rather than growth, though growth usually still happens unintentionally (56 percent in 2020 without any paid marketing or outbound sales). Managing for stability rather than growth is unusual in the software industry. As a result, we have had to come up with our own tools and ways of setting goals. I present this as one example of how you might use customer research to meet revenue goals.

Twice a year, I download all of our revenue data, take the top 80 percent of our revenue, and then analyze that basket like a portfolio manager would a portfolio of stocks. I look at it primarily by industry and company size, and layer in things like revenue volatility from that customer and industry type. As a horizontal product that sells to a wide variety of industries and company sizes, this analysis gives us a high-level view of our customer base.

I then try to speak with as many of those top 80 percent customers as I can.

I might also focus on a specific segment. For example, a few years ago we realized 20 percent of revenue was coming from real estate, and that felt high to us. After all, if our customer base were a stock portfolio that was being managed for stability, that would be too much from one industry or asset class. So, we set a goal of increasing customers in financial services and healthcare, which had thus far been quite sticky but were a much lower percentage of customers. We set a goal of increasing customers in those two industries. To do that, we needed to figure out why people in those industries were choosing us and what other options they were considering. I interviewed all of our customers in those industries, in addition to competitor research and overall market position research. As a result of the interviews, we were able to uncover the value of features in their contexts, add marketing that spoke to those specific needs and market environments, and adapt how we delivered our products.

The end result? Financial services and health were our largest-gaining industry customer segments in 2020.

NOTES

1. EMPATHY IS A LEARNABLE SKILL

1. Morgan Housel, *The Psychology of Money*, page 109
2. *I Thought It Was Just Me (But It Isn't)*, page 33
3. Chris Voss, *Never Split the Difference*, page 72
4. (*I Thought It Was Just Me (But It Isn't)*, page 37)
5. Interview by the author with Theodora Chu, 6/21/2021
6. https://www.uxmatters.com/mt/archives/2016/03/excuses-excuses-why-companies-dont-conduct-user-research.php

2. THE NEUROSCIENCE OF LISTENING

1. *Scientific American*, "The Neuroscience of Everybody's Favorite Topic" by Adrian F. Ward, July 16, 2013. deployempathy.com/ward

3. WHY I WROTE THIS BOOK

1. Interview by the author with Theodora Chu, 6/21/2021
2. See Brene Brown's *I Thought It Was Just Me (But It Isn't)* and Marshall B. Rosenberg's *Nonviolent Communication*.

5. HOW THIS BOOK IS STRUCTURED

1. Interview by the author with Theodora Chu, 6/21/2021

6. EVERYTHING IS A PROCESS

1. https://www.grandviewresearch.com/industry-analysis/laundry-detergent-pods-market
2. https://think.design/user-design-research/five-whys/

9. VALUABLE, USABLE, VIABLE, AND FEASIBLE

1. Marty Cagan is widely regarded as one of the leading thinkers on digital product management and development. See his book *Inspired* for more on this framework.

10. YOU—YES YOU—CAN DO THIS

1. https://twitter.com/amrancz/status/1372822035919933441

14. INTERVIEWS OR NUMBERS?

1. Interview between the author and Theodora Chu, 6/21/2021

15. PROJECT-BASED RESEARCH

1. Interview between the author and Theodora Chu, 6/21/2021
2. Interview between the author and Theodora Chu, 6/21/2021
3. Interview between the author and Theodora Chu, 6/21/2021

16. HOW MANY PEOPLE SHOULD YOU TALK TO?

1. http://deployempathy.com/voc
2. http://deployempathy.com/nielsen
3. Text conversation between the author and Derek Featherstone; https://twitter.com/feather/status/1387077149388156933

18. ONGOING RESEARCH

1. Erika Hall, *Just Enough Research*, page 11
2. See *Thinking Fast and Slow*.

20. TWITTER

1. deployempathy.com/sales-safari
2. Scott Hurff, a *Sales Safari* alum, discusses the *Sales Safari* method in depth in his book *Designing Products People Love*.

21. LINKEDIN

1. deployempathy.com/linkedin

25. USE A GENTLE TONE OF VOICE

1. Chris Voss, *Never Split the Difference*, page 31

27. LEAVE PAUSES FOR THEM TO FILL

1. For an introduction to Dr. Tannen's work, listen to the Hidden Brain episode "Why Conversations Go Wrong." deployempathy.com/hiddenbrain
2. See Dr. Robert Cialdini's *Influence* or listen to episode 463 of *Freaknomics Radio*, "How to Get Anyone to Do Anything" https://freakonomics.com/podcast/frbc-robert-cialdini/

28. MIRROR AND SUMMARIZE THEIR WORDS

1. Chris Voss, *Never Split the Difference*, page 56

29. DON'T INTERRUPT

1. Chris Voss, *Never Split the Difference*, page 16

38. INTERVIEW PREPARATION

1. Jim Kalbach, *The Jobs to Be Done Playbook*, page 71
2. deployempathy.com/nugget
3. https://deployempathy.com/heiter/

39. HOW CAN I EVALUATE THIS IDEA?

1. Mike Rogers, "Saying Goodbye to Typo CI," May 23 2021. deployempathy.com/rogers

40. WHY DID THEY BUY?

1. deployempathy.com/klement

45. THE "REACHING FOR THE DOOR" QUESTION

1. Steve Portigal, *Interviewing Users*, page 80.

47. DEBUGGING INTERVIEWS

1. *Lean Customer Development*, page 57

48. DRAWING A SIMPLE CUSTOMER JOURNEY MAP

1. For more on journey mapping, see *Service Design: From Insight to Inspiration* by Andy Polaine, Ben Reason, and Lavrans Løvlie and *The Jobs to Be Done Playbook* by Jim Kalbach.
2. Interview by the author with Theodora Chu, 6/21/2021

49. THE PAIN AND FREQUENCY MATRIX

1. See *Intercom on Jobs to Be Done* by Des Traynor.
2. Des Traynor, "Not All Good Products Make Good Businesses," August 15, 2016. I probably recommend this blog post to founders once a week. It's worth reading and bookmarking. deployempathy.com/traynor

50. SAMPLE INTERVIEW TRANSCRIPT

1. This is the overall goal: "Build a job listing platform."
2. Specific step in the process related to the product
3. Next step in the process related to the product
4. Customer's conceptualization of the activity ("problem"), and also the functional dimension
5. Firebase Storage is a tool to store images, PDFs, and other files.
6. If a website were a restaurant, the database would be the pantry.
7. This is a case-in-point example of the value of the process-based approach for which this book advocates: discover the different steps of a process and solve adjacent steps that would otherwise require multiple products
8. Next.js is a front-end framework that talks to the browser and displays the website to the user.
9. This is an example of using the customer's words and phrases. Note that he uses "walls" and "jumping through a lot of hoops" and I use those words in my follow-up.
10. He offered a specific example himself, but often, you have to dig for an example. Always dig for a specific example when something happened.
11. Step in the process
12. This is labeling the emotion to elicit elaboration.

13. Trying to gauge the Switch timeline for when he became aware of the issue and started considering something else.
14. This is an example of summarizing incorrectly to elicit elaboration.
15. Labeling
16. Emotional dimension
17. Still trying to build out that Switch timeline.
18. Jobs to Be Done literature talks about the four forces around switching products: things that externally push someone towards a new solution, things that intrinsically pull them towards it, anxieties about switching, and inertia/habit that keep them in place. This is an example of anxiety.
19. Firestore is a database. If a website were a restaurant, the database would be the pantry.
20. Looking for "What else have they tried?"
21. From the Four Forces perspective, this is inertia of the current solution
22. This is a pull towards something new: he wanted it to work, and it didn't, and that created disappointment which in turn created openness to something new.
23. Labeling
24. This is an example of asking for clarification even when it may not be necessary. One could guess what he meant by "paywall," yet I intentionally asked for clarification.
25. This is a clue to the broader situational context. He had limited time for this project and didn't want to spend it trying to figure out pricing models.
26. This is an example of summarizing.
27. This is building the timeline to figure out the path he went on to switch products. (See the Switch Interview Script for more.)
28. Ruby is a server-side programming language. "Ruby" is often used interchangeably with "Ruby on Rails," the most popular Ruby framework. Extending the analogy of a website as a restaurant, the French *brigade de cuisine* for organizing the roles of the kitchen is like a framework. Frameworks make writing code easier and more organized (for the most part).
29. Understanding the decision process to look for marketing/onboarding opportunities
30. A Code Pen is a way to demo code before installing it. A code test drive, if you will.
31. Amazon S3 is another way of storing files and images. It is often referred to as just "S3."
32. Labeling
33. This is the point when one may be tempted to say something to the effect of "Wow that's amazing!" (which congratulates the user) or "I'm so glad to hear that!" (which centers the interviewer and not the interviewee). If you're the product creator, you might need to let yourself privately have that moment of joy that they were happy with it, but remind yourself to hold it in and ask a question that digs deeper.
34. Digging for social factors behind the use of tools and who else may have been involved in the decision.
35. Trying to see if there were other decision-makers involved.
36. Moving on to gauging satisfaction with the product.
37. This is the Reaching For the Door Question.
38. This is an example of responding to a feature request. Some people intentionally distance themselves from products they build in an effort to get more honest

responses. If you are building the product, you can skip to "We've heard that from other people. I'm curious, could you say more about what leads your organization to need that?"

39. Clarifying the process
40. Digging for a specific situation.

52. QUICK ANALYSIS

1. For more on interview analysis, see *Service Design, Mental Models,* and *The Jobs to Be Done Playbook.*
2. Amazon S3 is another way of storing files and images. It is often referred to as just "S3."

58. CUSTOMER SUPPORT

1. Credit to copywriter Jebra Turner for this turn of phrase, which she herself heard from a scion of her local business community.

THANKS

This may be a self-published book, but it was not a solo effort.

I first want to thank my family. My husband, Mathias, who is my life partner, business partner, parenting partner, and partner in everything else. You read every word of this book when it was just a newsletter and are a source of unending support and believe in me more than I could ever believe in myself. I love you. Sophie, thank you for your enthusiasm and support. I love you. To Nigel, who curls up under my feet while I'm working and is the sweetest dog I could ever ask for.

Colleen Schnettler, my podcast cohost, work wife, and friend. Our conversations directly sparked this book. This never would have happened without your encouragement.

Holly Fake, Betsy Bland, and Blake Bos: I never would have started on my journey into user research without you, and I'm so grateful our paths crossed. You are my user research brain trust and have been such patient teachers and collaborators over the years.

The Bbiz squad: y'all are my cheerleaders, support group, and sounding board. I'm so grateful to have met you all.

Nicole Kaeding, Laurie Ohlstein, and Gabriel Chuan, who gave me honest word-by-word feedback on multiple drafts. You made it better, and I'm grateful for you.

To Pete and Jennifer, who taught me how to show empathy to myself.

To all of the alpha readers of this book who let me interview you about customer interviewing (so meta!), each one of you provided valuable feedback and encouragement: Aditya Rao, Stefan Manku, Pavel Ivanovsky, Sebastian Rao, Jonathan Markwell, Cam Sloan, Robert Balazsi, Benedicte Raae, Alex Wagner, Jebra Turner, Damien Terwagne, Dan Treacy, Hemedi Saidi, Adam McCrea, Josh Frank, Michael Christofides, George Stocker, JT Booth, Bruno Bornsztein, Ben Aldred, Darian Moody, Shawn Wang, Joy Heron, Vic Vijayakumar, Chisa Koiwa, Vivek Ranjan, Lili Kastilio, and Hua Shu. Thank you for making time to talk to me, for reviewing early drafts and giving detailed feedback, and for letting me ask "Can you say more about that?" even when you knew exactly what I was doing.

Thank you to Theodora Chu, who let me turn the tables and interview her about user research at Stripe.

To my Founder Summit group: Daniel Sim, Johnny Platt, Karsten Rasmussen, Chris Forster, Gregory Cronie, Steny Solitude, and Dean Layton-James. Our conversations were a seed for this book.

To my proofreader Ray Sylvester, who expediently flagged many typos.

To Arvid Kahl and Sean Fioritto, who generously shared their own self-publishing journeys with me and answered many questions.

To the hundreds of alpha readers who left anonymous feedback over many early drafts and replied with comments to the first-cut rough drafts published in my newsletter: thank you. Your enthusiasm from the earliest days made this project happen and kept me going.

ABOUT THE AUTHOR

Michele Hansen is an entrepreneur. She co-founded a software-as-a-service company, Geocodio, with her husband Mathias in 2014. Geocodio started as a small side project that made $31 its first month. Michele and Mathias grew Geocodio through revenue alone and Michele went full-time on the business in 2017. Prior to Geocodio, Michele was a product manager in financial publishing and a technical project manager at a web development agency.

She is also part of the *Software Social* podcast, which she co-hosts with Colleen Schnettler. *Software Social* was a finalist for Best Podcast, Best Hosts, and Best Episode in the 2020 SaaS Podcast Awards.

Michele is a frequent guest on other podcasts and has spoken at MicroConf and Laracon.

Originally from the US, she lives with her husband, daughter and dog on a small farm in the Danish countryside. She enjoys reading, adult gymnastics, and talking to people about talking to people.

You can find her on Twitter at twitter.com/mjwhansen, subscribe to the *Deploy Empathy* newsletter at deployempathy.com/newsletter, and email her at michele@deployempathy.com.

Made in the USA
Middletown, DE
19 September 2021

48616841R00186